The High-Value Writing Workbook:

Write for Success in Work and Life

by

Erin Lebacqz

For permission to quote or excerpt material, or to request bulk orders, please contact support@highvaluewriting.com.

Editing by Skylar Griego

Cover and Interior Design by Guy Rogers

ISBN 979-8-9906649-6-8 (paperback)

Printed in the United States of America

The High-Value Writing Workbook: Write for Success in Work and Life

Introduction:
The Two Goals of Intentional Writing

A few years ago, I emailed a collaborator a list of ideas we could use for an upcoming project. The list was long and descriptive, but I was optimistic: My work partner was going to be so excited that I'd come up with so many ideas for us!

Wrong.

Days went by and he didn't respond. Did he not like my ideas at *all?* I wondered. Was he just not bothering to respond?

Fast forward a few more days to our next collaborative meeting. Despite the lack of response, I still hopped onto the video call with anticipation. Maybe my associate had already spent time processing my ideas and would bring his responses to the meeting!

Wrong again.

"Um…" he began, looking a little unsure how to begin.

"Yes?" I encouraged. "What is it?"

"Um… That was… a *lot* of ideas, Erin," he finally stated. And then he went on to bring up something else, and we moved on to another topic.

It became clear to me: He hadn't even read all my ideas.

In situations like this, it can be tempting to blame the reader. The ideas were all written down—why not just *read* them?

But I've come to believe that we as writers also bear some of the responsibility for whether our writing gets read. In my case, I'd focused so much on my own desire to share information that I hadn't even considered what it might be like to *receive* all that text.

I'd forgotten about the human on the other side.

I'd forgotten that writing—much like speaking—is actually interactive.

If I wanted to create positive outcomes from this written interaction, I was going to have to think about more than just my own long lists of ideas and information.

I'd have to start considering more than what I'll call the informational goals of my writing; I'd also have to work toward the relational goals of every message I write.

Most of the learning we do about writing happens in school, where we learn to write to show what we know—and to get judged for it. Academic writing taught us to reflect, persuade, support ideas with evidence, and more. The writing we did in school helped us learn to write toward informational goals like clarity, evidence-based persuasion, and structure.

But one thing was missing from the type of writing we did in school: a true reader—someone who needed to not only read what we've written, but immediately understand it, and even use our message to take action. Because we didn't have this kind of reader for our academic writing, we didn't get a chance to learn about the relational goals of writing.

The relational goals of our writing include considerations like tone, trust, respect, and even the power dynamics that may come through in our writing. These aspects of our writing can impact our relationships with our readers. Thinking about our relational goals helps us not only inform—but connect with—our readers.

If you're at work, you're probably not writing for you. Unless you're note-taking or journaling, your writing actually exists for someone else. In our personal lives, too, we write for others: leaving notes, sending texts—even emailing family and friends, sports teams, and kids' clubs. To succeed with this kind of writing, we need to write with others in mind.

 Writing for Others

Put a checkmark next to the readers or audiences you write to on a regular basis.

- ❑ Family and friends
- ❑ Members of a club or team
- ❑ My supervisor
- ❑ My team members
- ❑ My direct reports
- ❑ Peers or colleagues
- ❑ Others inside my organization
- ❑ Others outside my organization
- ❑ Leadership
- ❑ The public
- ❑ Community members
- ❑ Parents, teachers, staff at kids' schools.

In most writing situations, you may be the creator of your writing, but someone on the previous checklist is the *user* of that writing. To write strategically—to meet our goals through intentionally-chosen words—we can't focus on ourselves. We need to combine informational and relational goals when we write to and for other people.

I've been teaching writing for decades, and that includes observing participants in my classes—their writing styles, their expectations when they're reading other people's messages, and which writing strategies they find most empowering. I've heard their stories and learned about their writing successes and their writing fails.

Far and away, the most consistent message is this:

> In work and real-life situations, writing that meets both informational and relational goals helps people succeed.

People who write with both sets of goals in mind create balanced writing that works for their reader. They're both concise and nice. They don't over-inform or under-inform. They hit the right tone. They come off as professional and thoughtful because they've thought about the human being on the other side.

Writing toward both informational and relational writing goals helps people write with intention and empathy—and it shows. The reader feels "seen" and therefore more likely to respond positively to a message. When we write toward both informational and relational goals, we get to simultaneously inform and connect with our reader.

INFORMATIONAL AND RELATIONAL WRITING GOALS
Informational and relational writing goals often include considerations like:

Informational (I) Goals:	*Relational (R) Goals:*
clarity, concision, completion, instruction	tone, voice, attitude, power dynamics, trust, respect

This workbook will focus on ways you can meet both sets of writing goals at once. We'll look at strategies for writing clearly and concisely and for building trust and managing relationships. By meeting both goals simultaneously in our writing, we can accomplish complex goals like:

- Getting our information read (I) by readers facing stress and content overload (R)
- Disagreeing with someone's idea (I) without hurting the relationship (R)
- Advocating for ourselves (I) without overlooking our reader's needs (R)
- Criticizing or redirecting (I) a team member without losing trust (R)

Writing to meet both sets of goals simultaneously doesn't have to be hard. By using some practical writing strategies, and developing self-awareness around our own writing habits, we can create writing that gets read and responded to positively.

And success comes from there. With strong, intentional writing, we not only work to meet our business and personal goals but also build and maintain strong relationships in the process.

Writing with intention in a remote world

Today, most of us write in multiple ways for our jobs and careers. This might include emails, texts, posts, comments on posts, direct messages, and conversations in project-sharing platforms. In all of these cases, our writing represents us. It stands in for us when we can't reply to something in person or on the phone. And it's often the very first step in forming a relationship.

In a post-pandemic world, this is even more true. You may have professional relationships with people you've never met in person or spoken to on the phone. I know I do. And because we more often present ourselves for the first time through an email or other written introduction, we have even more goals for our writing now. We can now use our writing to positively influence perceptions, actions, behaviors, and relationships.

Writing in a Remote World
Put a checkmark next to the statements that describe you.

❑ I often write to people I've never met and will never meet.

❑ I often read messages from people I've never met and will never meet.

❑ I mainly write to people I already know.

❑ I mainly write to people I can also talk to on the phone or in the office.

❑ Sometimes I get a sense of what the writer's like from reading their writing.

❑ Sometimes I worry about what feelings about me the reader might get from my writing.

Imagine you receive an email in which the writer introduces themselves for the first time, and asks you to consider meeting with them in an advisory capacity. I'd wager you might form different opinions of this person depending on which of the following they sent you:

- "Can we meet? You seem like a great mentor and I need one."
- "I need a mentor. When are you available?"
- "Do you have any time to meet next week? I'm new and would appreciate your time."
- "I'm new to the field and need a mentor. Can you help me?"
- "As a first-year employee, I'm looking to learn from others with more experience. Would you have time for a one-hour meeting in the next month?"

Based on the above examples, I can imagine myself saying "Yes" or saying "No," depending. For me, the issue is the focus: Is the writer self-centered, or did they consider *my* needs too? For example, the second statement respects my time more than the first, in my opinion. Many of us tend to form opinions of others based on whether they behave according only to the needs of themselves, or consider the greater collective to at least some extent.

Writing to meet reader needs

I recently spoke with someone for whom this tendency was even more important: a landlord who based decisions about who got to rent his various apartments on the ways applicants texted him. We met in the coffee shop in Sacramento where I do much of my work. Since I'm a writing teacher, he approached me with a writing story. Here's about how it went:

"You teach writing!" he declared one day.

"Indeed I do," I responded. I'm never sure where this kind of thing is going to go.

"Do you help people write better texts?"

"Sometimes, yes. Most of the same principles that apply to workplace writing like email also apply to writing texts," I answered.

"So true," he said, and then proceeded to explain his approach to reading the texts of those who applied to rent his various properties.

"I judge them partially just on how they write their texts," he continued.

"Really?" I asked, concerned. "You mean spelling and stuff? That doesn't seem too fair to me; not everyone has had the same education."

"No no no," the landlord replied, with waves of his hands wiping away the thought. "I judge them on whether they address what I've asked in my texts, or whether they simply ignore my needs and just text all about themselves."

My curiosity was piqued.

"I figure," he continued, "that if they can't respond to what another person needed in a simple text when applying to even get the apartment, then how will they be as a tenant? Potentially super self-focused? Potentially not attentive to what we ask of them? Potentially, then, not super considerate of neighbors even."

Of course, the error on the part of the texter could have been accidental. We don't want to appear disrespectful in our writing; it's just hard to think about everything, and the reader's potential interpretation. And yet our writing does stand in for us when we aren't there. It comes to represent us or put forward an image of "what we're like"—and it's only human.

Writing isn't just about "correctness." It's about clarity, consideration, and emotional intelligence. We have so much to balance in our writing. While we do need to inform our reader of our own needs, we also want to write in a way that respects our reader and considers theirs.

This workbook, then, will help you balance *both* aspects of our writing goals: informational and relational. We'll look at easy strategies for writing more clearly and concisely. We'll also look at ways to ensure your reader feels respected. I'll bring in advice I've learned from the thoughtful people in my live sessions—advice about what real readers want.

Using this workbook

My hope is that this workbook will be easy to use independently, but also feel sort of interactive. I'll share stories and "before and after" examples, and then offer strategies to practice on your own. I'll be there with you in spirit as you practice the revision exercises.

You may find some of the sentences in the practice problems a little general, or even generic. I chose not to write example sentences for specific industries as that might exclude readers from other industries. My hope is that you can take a strategy we practice with general examples and apply it to your specific work afterward.

Relatedly, this workbook lacks an answer key. The revisions and reflections the exercises ask for simply don't have "right" answers. In general, there isn't a "right" way to write anyway. What's "right" always depends on the situation and circumstance—including who will read our writing, and what we're trying to accomplish with that writing.

As you work through the practical high-value writing strategies in this book, then, consider the situations behind the various examples. "What would work best in this situation?" is a great thing to ask yourself when revising writing.

You'll also find a few supplemental learning opportunities referenced throughout the workbook:

Watch + Learn

When an idea aligns with a video from the High-Value Writing YouTube channel, you'll find a QR code that'll take you right to that video. Consider watching the video while working on a particular section if you like learning through video instruction. For example, the QR code to the right takes you to a video that welcomes you to the workbook and helps you get started!

Goes with ...

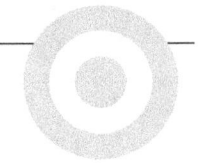

When a particular idea aligns with content I've covered in my book *High-Value Writing: Real Strategies for Real-World Writing,* you'll find reference to the partner pages. Reading the book isn't necessary for using this workbook. But partnering the book and the workbook can take your learning even further. Look for this symbol ⊙ and turn to the referenced pages in the *High-Value Writing: Real Strategies for Real-World Writing* book.

Thoughts?

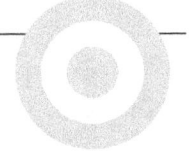

You'll also find space for note-taking on the right-hand side of the narrative portions of this book. Many of these areas are labeled with "Thoughts?" and the target symbol, as seen to the right. I'd encourage you to use this space to write down key points you're learning, reminders for yourself, and ideas on how and where to apply these strategies in the writing you do in your job and life.

Finally, you'll find opportunities to reflect and revise throughout this workbook. The icons below will indicate the type of activity or exercise, as follows:

 analyzing and highlighting ideas, words, or phrases

 reflecting on your writing and the people you write to

 thinking about, planning, and ordering your writing

 revision and practice, "before and after" exercises

 chapter review, identifying action items

So, let's get into it! Chapter 2 will launch our writing practice with strategies on writing concisely, but also nicely. After that, we'll get into more writing strategies for creating clear, connected writing. First, though, Chapter 1 will ask you to reflect on your writing habits, strengths, and opportunities for growth. By knowing ourselves as writers, we can more easily target areas we'd like to improve on and build confidence from there.

1

Your Writing Defaults:
Reflecting on Your Writing Style and Goals

Before we start talking about how to create clear, connected writing, let's check in about our current writing styles and habits. By knowing ourselves as writers, we can better know what we're already good at—and what to work on.

Most of us have various habits we've developed for our writing. I like to call these "writing defaults." Knowing our default behaviors helps us know how and when we may need to adapt our writing for particular readers— or to meet particular goals. For example, if we know we tend to give lots of detail, we can adjust that amount depending on what a given reader would want or need.

Or, if a writer defaults to a very formal tone, this writer can stick with their default when writing to readers in very formal industries, companies, or cultures. But that same writer can know to adjust when they're writing to a reader who might find a very formal tone off-putting.

Below, you'll find two self-assessment exercises about your writing habits and one about your readers. Work your way through these activities thinking about the way your writing turns out by default *before* editing. Then, take a moment to reflect on whether you'd like to adapt any of these habits to be a more strategic writer.

 Identifying Your Writing Habits
Put a checkmark next to any writing habits you tend to "default" to:

❑ Provide a lot of detail.

❑ Provide little detail.

❑ Write in a wordy style.

❑ Write in a direct style.

❑ Use a casual tone.

❑ Use a formal tone.

❑ Sound very direct.

❑ Sound somewhat indirect.

❑ Sound confident.

❑ Sound like I'm not confident.

❑ Write run-on sentences or in a "stream of consciousness" style.

❑ Use a lot of fragments.

❑ Sound slightly "bureaucratic."

❑ Write long paragraphs.

❑ Use lots of bullets and/or other design/layout elements.

❑ Other: _____

❑ Other: _____

 Considering Your Writing Style

Rank yourself from 1–5 on the following five writing habit spectrums:

Wordy	1	2	3	4	5	Concise
"Business Only"	1	2	3	4	5	Friendly
Formal	1	2	3	4	5	Informal
Over-informative	1	2	3	4	5	Under-informative
Very Organized	1	2	3	4	5	Unstructured

This third self-assessment asks you to consider how much you typically think about your reader. Sometimes when we write, we just start writing. But when we stop and think about our reader first, we can fine tune our writing intentionally to help us meet our goals.

Ways I Think about My Reader

Mark the ideas you usually consider when you email, text, or otherwise "message" your reader.

❑ What do they need to know?

❑ What do they not need to know?

❑ How much detail will they want?

❑ How formal should I sound?

❑ How long should this be?

❑ How can I make my message stand out and get read?

❑ Other _____

❑ Other _____

Now, consider whether there's anything you'd like to intentionally alter about your writing habits. For example, I've had to adapt my tendency to provide many, many ideas in one message. Now, when I write to someone, I only include the ideas that pertain to the specific matter at hand. I hold back my other ideas, and then share them later if they become relevant.

In the spaces below, record a few goals for your writing. You may also want to come back to this section once you've done some of the activities in this book. Reflecting on your writing goals in this way actually helps you make progress toward meeting them!

Adapting My Writing Habits to Help My Readers

Record a few ideas below, listing habits you'd like to adapt.

1. _____

2. _____

3. _____

4. _____

Whenever I teach a live session for a professional client, I provide a self-assessment survey about their writing goals before our session. Participants are asked to identify areas of writing they feel confident about and areas they hope to improve on during the workshops.

Far and away, the most common response to the latter is something like this: "I'm wordy and want to be more concise." Or, "I'd like to be both concise and nice."

I'm the same way. Based on the thousands of people to whom I've presented this question, I'd say about 75% of us wish we were more concise. The remaining 25% often tell me they are very clear and direct, but that some readers have mentioned they sound "harsh."

How can we strike a balance between very direct and friendly, personable writing? By writing with intention, of course! Let's get started.

Chapter

2

Concise and Nice:
Writing Clear, Concise, Courteous Messages

The first thing to know about today's readers is that they're busy. But you already knew that! You're one of them, and you're busy too. You may know first-hand how difficult it can be to focus on what one's reading these days, given all the surrounding "noise." I know I do.

Between ever-increasing responsibilities and the growth of content overload among most of our population, we need to consider a reader's mental bandwidth when we write. Overloading our reader won't help us meet our goals because our reader may not be able to respond effectively.

Brain research has shown that our minds can only manage a finite amount of information at a time. If our reader's already stressed, dealing with an overwhelming schedule and potentially overloaded mind, they may only be able to fit so many more thoughts in. In a social context of busy readers, how can we make our writing stand out, get read, and even get responded to or acted on?

As we discuss strategies for both informing and connecting with your reader, we'll consider this reality of content overload. By writing concisely, making our writing scannable, and considering our reader's needs, we can increase the chances our reader will read and respond to the messages we send them.

To cut through the noise our busy readers face each day, it helps when we:

- focus on meaning over words
- lead with *who* and *what* information
- use visual verbs that create concision and set the right tone
- use concise verbs over wordy nouns when possible
- avoid slow lead-ins and get right to the action

Thoughts?

Writing concisely means focusing on meaning over words

Much of our past learning about writing has focused on words more than on meaning. We hear a lot about writing "correctly," but not as much about how to intentionally create meaning—or create perceptions or even behaviors in our readers.

Goes with 20-21

For many of us, school may have been the last time we talked at length about writing. In school, we were asked to create paragraphs and essays using well-chosen words—a lot of them. We learned guidelines that helped us get through school, but while some of these guidelines also apply to workplace writing, others don't.

At work, time is of the essence, and that includes reading time. To hone our message and save our readers time, we need to focus on providing more meaning in fewer words—not the other way around. We need to write in a way that's *meaning-forward,* or *frontloads* meaning for our readers.

The first step to writing concisely, then, is to recognize when we're providing meaning through our writing—and when we're just providing words. That's right: It's possible to write a whole lot of words, but still convey little meaning. That's something we want to avoid.

The examples below will further illustrate and explain this concept. You'll find the lower-meaning words *italicized,* to point out words that add to the word count without really contributing much, and word counts in parenthesis.

LESS MEANING, MORE WORDS	MORE MEANING, LESS WORDS
It is important to note the impact hybrid work *may have had.* (12)	Let's look at possible hybrid work impacts. (7)
This is to inform you that there will be an announcement from leadership tomorrow listing the new classes. (18)	Leadership will announce the new classes tomorrow. (7)
The candidates *for the position were asked* to submit a writing sample *as part of their interview.* (17)	We asked interview candidates to submit a writing sample. (9)

To make our writing concise, we need to use words higher in meaning—and fewer of them. This also means recognizing words or phrases that don't convey meaning, but only increase our word count and work against concision.

In a few pages, we'll start working with specific strategies that make your writing more concise. Before that, however, let's take a moment to practice recognizing lack of meaning when we see it.

Recognizing words that don't add meaning

Underline/highlight passages that provide words, but don't necessarily add to the message's actual meaning.

1. There are a few reasons we would like to recommend adding a second assistant.

2. It is important to note the requirements listed at the top of this page.

3. It is a requirement that all operators have received a level C2 training.

4. It has come to our attention that your file is in need of updating.

5. Based on employee survey results, it is clear that it would be popular to offer more opportunities around technology training.

As you worked through the examples above, you probably noted the way some words actually give lots of information, while other words are just… there. In some cases, you may have highlighted or underlined nearly the whole sentence!

To write concisely, let's avoid low-meaning words and focus on writing that truly informs and connects us with our readers. By getting important meaning to our reader quickly, we increase the chances they'll find what they need right away—and continue reading.

To write concisely, lead with Who + What

The easiest way to write concisely is to write in a way that's meaning-forward. By opening our sentences with the most important information, we inform our reader right away. This means busy readers don't have to wait to learn the information they need. And it means less editing for us—even, eventually, zero editing!

Let's revisit the five sentences we analyzed for meaning previously. All of these sentences could have been meaning-forward with a simple reorganization.

In fact, anytime you're facing a really long, wordy sentence and don't feel like editing, you don't actually have to. Instead, just reorder the concepts in your wordy sentence to lead with **Who** is doing something (subject or doer) and *What* they are doing (verb or action). This often means clarifying a **Who** that hasn't been previously identified (and is sometimes implied rather than directly stated). Here's how this might work:

Watch + Learn

Goes with 39-40

BEFORE	AFTER
There are a few reasons we would like to recommend adding a second assistant.	**We** *recommend* adding a second assistant for multiple reasons.
It is important to note the requirements listed at the top of this page.	**[You]** Please *note* the requirements at the top of the page.
It is a requirement that all operators have received a level C2 training.	All **operators** *must complete* level C2 training.
It has come to our attention that your file is in need of updating.	Your **file** *needs* to be updated. Or **[You]** Please *update* your file.
Based on employee survey results, it is clear that it would be popular to offer more opportunities around technology training.	Based on employee survey results, **we should offer** more technology training.

Leading with **Who** and *What* information basically guarantees you a concise sentence. And the best part? There's no need to edit by crossing out small words. Simply reorganize your sentence's words and concepts, and the fluff will fall away! Let's try out a few of these:

 ## Writing concisely by leading with Who + What

Reduce the length and fluff in the sentences below by revising to lead with Who + What.

BEFORE: It is listed on the application requirements that transcripts must be submitted by all candidates. (15)

AFTER: All candidates must submit transcripts to meet application requirements. (9)

1. It has come to our attention that you have not yet provided your emergency contact information.

   _____

2. It has not yet been decided whether we'll use Design A or Design B.

   _____

3. There are a few ways members can use the app to manage their finances.

   _____

4. It is a requirement that you submit new paperwork for each request.

   _____

5. I'm writing to inform you that our department requires a change of address form.

   _____

6. An announcement has been made by leadership that will have an impact on all vendors.

   _____

7. It is required by all operators on the floor that a safety training must be attended annually.

   _____

8. We have been informed that our medical staff has not yet received the supplies you sent.

   _____

9. It is with regret that we inform you of our early closing next week due to a water leak.

_____

10. It is required that you submit a cover letter and writing sample with your resume.

_____

These examples help illustrate why concise writing gets read more than wordy writing. If you're worried about your reader seeing your information, it helps to get that information out there right away! Leading with Who + What frontloads information to make things easy on your reader. Even a skimmer or scanner (more on that in Chapter 3) will likely see these important concepts at the very beginning of a sentence, bullet, or paragraph.

If you like studying grammar, you've noticed the above concept parallels the idea of using active voice. We'll revisit this idea later in the workbook, when we discuss intentionally *choosing* between active and passive voice for specific writing situations.

If you're not a grammar fan, don't worry. You can accomplish clear, concise writing by leading with Who + What, regardless!

Not all *Whats* help you write concisely

Although you'll always make sentences more concise by writing with a Who + What structure, you'll also want to carefully consider which "What" to use. While actions or verbs are typically our most meaning-full words, this isn't true for all of them.

Unlike strong, visual verbs, the verb "to be" typically creates fluff and works against concision. This verb includes commonly-used conjugations like *am, is, was, were,* and *will be;* as well as longer versions like *will have been.*

Examples include sentences like "She is the director" or "They were late for the final." Because the verb "to be" means little beyond... existing?... we'll usually need to bring in more words to set our meaning. That's when fluff potentially creeps in.

In most situations, we don't need to use a verb like *is* or *are.* Typically, we'll have other options—and those options will tend to be more concise. Consider these examples, which each include two versions: one using a "to be" verb and one using a visual verb. I'll italicize "to be" verbs (and

Watch + Learn

Goes with 32-33

surrounding fluff words required by those verbs) and list the word counts in parenthesis.

USING TO BE VERBS	USING VISUAL VERBS
Rebecca **was in charge of** that process last year. (9)	Rebecca **directed** that process last year. (6)
They **are going to vote on** the new process next week. (11)	They **will vote on** the new process next week. (9)
Praveet **was active in** mentorship last quarter with a new recruit. (13)	Praveet **mentored** a new recruit last quarter. (7)
Richard **is in favor of** the hybrid work option. (9)	Richard **prefers** the hybrid work option. (6)

We can see a few trends from the above examples. For one, while the sentences on the left include more words than those on the right, they don't necessarily provide more meaning. In fact, I'd argue in some cases it's the opposite.

For example, when Richard *prefers* the hybrid work option, we know there was at least one other option available. That's the extra information a strong, visual verb like *prefer* can bring. Similarly, learning Praveet *mentored* an employee includes more specifics than *was active in*.

To use visual verbs to increase concision, find longer strings of words surrounding "to be" verbs and then ask yourself: "Is there a verb for that?"

 ## Increasing concision by avoiding the verb "To Be"
Revise the sentences below by using a visual verb in place of the "to be" verb.

BEFORE: Sheila *is in support of* increasing outreach. (7)

AFTER: Sheila *supports* increasing outreach. (4)

1. Francesca **is opposed to** returning to the office full-time.

_____

2. My professor **is an advocate for** joining a union.

_____

3. The committee **is interested in** your feedback.

_____

4. Layla **was a candidate in** the race for mayor.

_____

5. After the session, evaluation forms **were received by** the participants.

_____

6. I knew Becky **was a huge sports fan** after she hosted three viewing parties.

_____

7. The final candidate we interviewed **is no longer interested in** the job.

_____

8. Before Ryan presents, I **am interested in** knowing a little more about his background.

_____

9. The new model **is a favorite among** lifelong hobbyists.

_____

10. For the new coding position, **there is a requirement that** you have two or more years of experience.

_____

Once you've tried these revisions, it's worth taking a look at your own writing habits again. Many of us default to using "is," "are," "was," or "were" in most of our sentences. Typically, it's a habit we picked up long ago. If you put a checkmark by this habit in Chapter 1, try focusing on using visual verbs and see how your writing transforms.

I'd also suggest doing a search through documents or emails you've written, to look for patterns. Enter "is" as a search term, for example, and see what you find. You'll probably notice the fluff words surrounding these empty verbs first. Then, figure out how often you use "to be" verbs and try keeping it to a minimum. This will naturally reduce your fluff and wordiness while increasing the meaning readers find in your writing.

Use verbs over nouns for clear, concise explanations

Take a look at the following pairs of sentences, and consider whether you find the (A) or (B) versions easier to read and comprehend.

A. These meetings tend to start a little late.
B. These meetings have a tendency to start a little late.

A. They were arguing in the hall.
B. They were having an argument in the hall.

A. She decided to apply.
B. She decided to submit her application.

Watch + Learn

Goes with 51–52

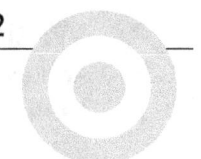

You might have noticed a few things in the pairs of sentences above. While the (A) sentences, for example, are a bit briefer, the (B) sentences provide the same information—but in a longer way. In all the examples, we get two ways of saying pretty much the same thing, but one's shorter. What's happening here?

Basically, the (A) sentences are shorter and potentially clearer because they center verbs. The (B) sentences, instead, put their meaning into a noun. There's a name for this: nominalization. This word basically means to "noun" something—to create a noun out of something.

So many concepts in English can be represented through either verbs or nouns. When we use the verb version, we tend to write more concisely. Here are a few more examples. Note the italicized *verb* in the first list, and italicized *noun* in the second.

Verb-focused	Noun-focused
They *agreed*.	They came to an *agreement*.
They *talked*.	They had a *conversation*.
We *applied*.	We submitted our *applications*.
Let's *conserve* energy.	Let's practice energy *conservation*.
We *planned*.	We made a *plan*.

In addition to being longer, the (B) sentences also include words with endings added to them. We see a lot of "-ment" words or "-tion" words in this list. To me, that implies the word was better off as a verb. Why extend the word into a noun that then requires more "helper words" to surround it? These words ending in "-ment" or "-tion" can also make our writing sound more bureaucratic.

When we're trying to sound "professional," we may tend to lean into the bureaucratic language that's been modeled to us in formal writing settings. We may accidentally start including more nominalizations than we'd typically use as a side effect of trying to sound official, "sophisticated," or correct.

To start using more verbs over nouns, look for the longer strings of words surrounding nouns that end in these suffixes. Ask yourself, "Is there a verb for that?" Chances are, there is. And by using the verb version, you'll reduce surrounding helper words like "had," "were," "a," "about," "on," and "to."

 Writing Concisely with Verbs over Nouns
Reduce sentence length by revising the sentences below to include a visual verb in place of a noun and its surrounding wordiness.

BEFORE: We have been asked to *make a modification to* this process.

AFTER: We have been asked to modify this process.

1. I overheard them *having a discussion about* the new protocol.

   _____

2. This team *has a tendency to* create multiple drafts.

   _____

3. We just wanted to *have a conversation about* it.

   _____

4. The updated procedures will help us *practice more energy conservation*.

   _____

5. Our new coach has asked that each family *make a contribution* each month.

   _____

6. We need to *submit a request for* more funding.

   _____

7. They *had a disagreement*.

   _____

8. Our Human Resources team *created a draft of* the new company values.

   _____

9. The weather *created an interference* with the reception.

_____

10. Our numbers *experienced growth*.

_____

Intentional, visual verbs help your writing be concise and nice

While most of us want to write more concisely, we also worry about balancing our clarity with courtesy. I receive questions about this often in live sessions or through the YouTube channel. People writing at work worry: "Won't extreme concision make me sound *harsh*?"

Because most readers are looking for clear, easy-access information, you're actually being courteous already when you write with concision. However, we can also take care to ensure our tone meets our relational goals by choosing our visual verbs with intention.

While visual verbs help increase concision in our writing, that's not the only thing they're good at. Visual verbs also help us set a tone. Therefore, we can be concise and nice by writing with a concise sentence structure, and then adjusting our nice tone through verb choice.

Visual verbs can impact the tone of our writing in all these ways and more:

- Give power and choice, or take power and choice away
- Create different levels of formality/informality and friendliness
- Make something sound engaging, boring, optional, or mandatory
- Convey a sense of consideration and respect—or fail to

I often use polls in live classes, asking participants to choose sentences that impact them in certain ways. In these situations, class participants are suddenly readers, reading and reacting to various sentences I've shown them. These readers react to various writing choices and vote on which sentence made them feel included, welcomed, required, or other impacts.

Watch + Learn

Goes with 31-32

The following example poll captures the power of intentional visual verbs:

"Which provides the warmest welcome?"

- Thank you for *attending*.
- Thank you for *joining* us.
- Thank you for *participating*.

In response to this kind of poll, participants will typically offer insights like these about the impacts of these visual verbs:

Attending	Joining	Participating
more formal	more together	more pressure
less choice	feel included	feel included
more bureaucratic	feel respected	
feel separate		

These examples remind us about the two sides of meaning: informational and relational. They also remind us we can meet two goals at once with our writing: informational goals and relational goals. I'd argue that all three of the above examples have almost the same exact informational meaning. However, their relational meaning varies quite a bit.

We can use visual verbs to adjust our tone and meet all kinds of relational goals with our writing. And we can do it while still remaining concise because all we need to do is adjust our visual verb. We don't need to add a second sentence to add courtesy.

Consider the differences in relational meaning among these various revisions:

- The committee *requests* your feedback.
- The committee *wants* your feedback.
- The committee *invites* your feedback.
- The committee *requires* your feedback.
- The committee *needs* your feedback.

Although all five sentences offer the same information meaning ("Feedback, please!"), their relational meanings vary. The committee and the feedback-giver gain and lose power and choice in the various revisions.

Let's work with a few of the ways visual verbs can impact relational meaning. In the next exercise, choose intentional visual verbs to ensure the revision meets the stated relational goal. In all cases, we'll remain concise since we're already using a concise sentence structure.

Impacting tone through intentional verb choice

Alter the tone of each sentence by intentionally choosing a new visual verb. It's also OK to reorganize the sentences by reordering words. Just make sure you use visual verbs in all the "action" spots!

BEFORE: I would like for us to *have a talk* in my office later today. (Make more friendly)

AFTER: Can you join me in my office to chat later today?

Make more formal:

1. We *want* you to join us.

   _____

2. The new manager *said* we'd start late.

   _____

3. Please *give* your feedback.

   _____

Make more informal:

4. We *request your presence at* our holiday dinner.

   _____

5. It *is a requirement that you submit an application* with three writing samples.

   _____

6. It *has been announced that* all employees are invited to attend.

   _____

Make more required:

7. We *want* your participation in Volunteer Days.

   _____

8. You're *invited to* complete this feedback form.

   _____

9. We *welcome* your expertise as we review this data.

   _____

Make more engaging or allow for choice (make more optional):

10. Please **attend** the session.

   _____

11. Our office requires that you provide an alternative account.

   _____

12. It is a **requirement that** you submit feedback on this process.

   _____

Make more friendly and respectful:

13. I have **solicited** feedback from each of you.

   _____

14. It **is required of** Lydia and Ron to complete the process.

   _____

15. Rafael **is now going to be the one** to tell us which recipe to follow.

   _____

Reduce slow lead-ins and get to the action to write with concision and impact

Have you ever received a message—maybe an email or a letter—beginning with "This is to inform you that..." and then going on to provide the message?

I have to confess: Sometimes, when I'm in this situation, I think to myself: "Well yes, I know this is to inform me—because I just received it!" It feels a little like stating the obvious.

And yet I too have found myself opening a message in this way.

Why do we do this? I believe it's because somewhere along the way, we picked up the idea that writing this way sounds "sophisticated" or even "professional." Our minds are like sponges, but in some cases, they may absorb the wrong thing. Because we've read slow lead-ins a lot in "professional" communication, our minds start to think it's the way to go.

However, as we've discussed, not all words inform our readers. Some words mean a lot; others mean a little. It's easy to fall into the habit of beginning sentences with a slow lead-in, later working up to the main point. However, this only confuses the reader and makes them wait for information.

Why delay giving information to someone who wants it? Why add words to our core message that may distract or even confuse our reader—delaying their responses as well?

Another way to be "concise and nice," then, is to avoid slow lead-ins. Instead of using slow lead-ins, we can get right to the core information: Who did something and what they did. By getting to the main point sooner, we can help our readers learn information more quickly and easily. By getting right to the action, we also sound more confident—a concept we'll discuss further in Chapter 10.

 Getting to the action without slow lead-ins
Revise the sentence to get to the action sooner, without slow lead-ins.
Keep in mind: keeping Who + What in the very front will make your sentence the most concise.

BEFORE: It has come to our attention that the team performed an audit on this data last year. (17)
AFTER: The team audited this data last year. (6)

BEFORE: There are seven products that we make available by delivery. (10)
AFTER: We deliver these seven products. (5)

1. This is to inform you that the letter you sent has been received by our office.

   _____

2. It is important to consider the reason she may have had.

   _____

3. There are a variety of options available to you when you choose a retirement plan.

   _____

4. I am writing to inform you that we are still waiting on you to upload your ID and Form D6 to your profile.

   _____

5. It has been brought to our attention that we have not yet received your application, which should be submitted through this link by Friday.

_____

6. It should be considered noteworthy that the panel includes two healthcare providers.

_____

7. It is a requirement of all applicants to submit two forms of government identification.

_____

8. There are a few ideas I can share about how to build your credit.

_____

9. It is a tradition among our team to hold a celebratory potluck at the end of the year.

_____

10. It has come to our attention that the remodeling quote you provided has expired.

_____

CONCISE AND NICE WRITING IN 3 STEPS

The above sections show us how to write clearly, concisely, and courteously at the same time. To do this every day in your professional writing, just run through these three steps to get there.

1. Revise a wordy sentence into a concise sentence by leading with Who + What.

   a. Make sure this includes getting rid of any slow lead-ins!

2. Ensure your What isn't a "to be" verb.

   a. If you've used a "to be" verb, replace it with a visual verb.

3. Replace your What with various synonyms until you find the one with your intended tone.

EXAMPLE

Original Sentence: This is to inform you that you have been asked to attend the reception.

1. You have been asked to attend the reception.
2. We ask you to attend the reception.
3. We invite you to attend the reception.

Key Takeaways & Action Items

You can use this page to record your most important insights, and keep track of the things you want to take action on. Reviewing and paraphrasing what you've learned will also help you remember and feel confident about what we've discussed and practiced.

Most impactful insights:

_____

_____

_____

Best strategies, tips, or tricks:

_____

_____

_____

Areas you'll apply these ideas (situations or types of documents/messages):

_____

One-sentence summary that captures the main point of this chapter:

_____

One word or phrase that captures the theme of this chapter: _____

"Before and After" Examples:

Before: _____

_____

After: _____

_____

Before: _____

_____

After: _____

_____

Chapter

3

Breaking through the Noise:
Writing to Get Read

I first met Florence in a two-day workshop she'd hired me to provide for her team. She was a learning director at a large federal organization.

Thoughts?

Florence shared with me that a few weeks ago, she'd emailed numerous members of her leadership team to advocate for new course topics she wanted to add to their offerings. A thoughtful writer, she'd included research and reasons, examples, and next steps. She wanted to make sure her readers knew why these course additions were a good idea—and whom they'd serve.

No one responded.

After the first day of my class, Florence decided to pivot. We'd been covering the "Now/Later/Never" strategy for detail management (coming up in this chapter), and she'd had an idea.

Florence went back to her original email—weighing in at about the equivalent of two pages—and analyzed each piece of information she'd shared. Then, she deleted everything her readers wouldn't immediately need to understand or respond to her message. Her email was now about three short paragraphs long. She sent it again and waited.

Two of her recipients responded *that day*.

Concise and nice writing helps us meet the needs of our readers by informing them quickly—and respecting them through our chosen tone. But using intentional word choice to get our messages read and acted upon doesn't stop there.

We can also make writing and design decisions that help control what our reader sees and reads, making sure they see what matters most. With a little intentional writing, we can actually steer the attention of our readers to or away from different ideas or information.

Writing concisely and writing with courtesy are, in many ways, the same thing. In today's professional setting, most of us read emails and other messages throughout the day—and give a lot of our time doing so. What could be more kind, in such a setting, than writing concisely?

But today's readers aren't just busy. Many of us also get overwhelmed with the content that's put in front of us to read and digest every day. This content overload creates busy, often cluttered minds. With so much to think about, we need clear, targeted writing to read. We need to get the message, know how to act on it, and move on.

To increase the likelihood that your central message gets seen, read, and responded to, consider making the information in your writing as accessible as possible by:

- using briefer, simpler words when possible
- making your messages as scannable as possible
- managing your reader's attention by using active and passive voice with purpose
- intentionally managing the level of detail in your writing

Using simple words makes reading easier and reduces misunderstandings

Our social histories around the world include times when not all of us were encouraged to get educated. Being allowed to attend school, and being able to afford it, separated people into groups—groups that were then given more, or less, opportunity. Schooling became worn as a badge of honor in some cases, showing other people that one had access to knowledge, power, and wealth.

When only some people get to access information, having that information can lead to economic and social power. A lofty vocabulary might be used to demonstrate one's education, power, or wealth. Groups who used words only they had been taught were in essence able to hold information hostage. By controlling access to information, they were better able to "maintain the status quo," or keep things as they were.

Today's readers aren't always super impressed by this kind of thing. Many of today's readers find it just a little bit *ostentatious*, or showy, when writers trot out the "impressive" vocabulary. I've even come to notice, through discussions in live classes, that it's become a sign of insecurity for some readers. "Why are they trying to impress me?" colleagues and customers find themselves asking.

Using "million-dollar vocab words" can also risk making a writer look like they're seeking or clinging to power. Just like medical jargon can alienate patients or "legalese" can intimidate a witness, writing with "big words" can look like a power play.

To help readers struggling with content overload, we can use the simpler, shorter synonyms of longer words instead. By using familiar, everyday words, we can imagine our readers' brains taking a relaxing moment after all the mental clutter we build up going through a typical day.

When this concept comes up in a live workshop or webinar, a participant will often ask: "Will simplifying my language make me look less smart?" Years of myths about writing have made us think we only look smart if we show readers the very best vocabulary we're capable of.

Reminder, though: that's not always strategic. In goal-based writing, like the writing we want to do at work, we're trying to get something done when we write. Remember the idea of two sets of simultaneous writing goals? Here's how the two sides of this debate stack up in response to writing to meet both informative and relational goals:

WRITING WITH LONGER, MORE DECORATIVE WORDS	WRITING WITH SHORTER, MORE FAMILIAR WORDS
Informative goal: We hope they have time to read/understand.	**Informative goal:** They're more likely to read/understand.
Relational goal: They're either impressed or they're annoyed. Want to gamble?	**Relational goal:** Your words are more welcoming, less alienating.

Unless you know your audience will appreciate it, using decorative words may not be worth the risk. Based on the above comparison, we have a better chance of getting read and a better chance at developing a strong relationship with our reader by using accessible language. We also wipe out the risk of sounding either showy or insecure.

Let's try this out. As we study writing with accessible words, we'll start by simply replacing some longer words with shorter synonyms.

 Increasing Readability through Familiar Word Choice
Make the following sentences more accessible by replacing the more complex words in italics with simpler synonyms.

BEFORE: We will now *demonstrate* the *modifications*.

AFTER: We will now show you the changes.

1. To increase *camaraderie* among our employees, it is recommended that managers consider *the application of interactive strategies* in meetings.

2. Our *protocol requires* that users *demonstrate* lack of *negative environmental impact.*

3. It is *incumbent* upon the user to consider the safety *protocol*.

_____

4. Leaders should *demonstrate propriety* when *addressing* personal issues with *personnel*.

_____

5. *Prior to* the vote, it is *crucial to ensure* that board members are *provided with sufficient* background on the topic.

_____

6. Machine operators *should avoid referencing outdated* work instructions.

_____

7. *Utilize* caution when *anticipating* opening the fume hood.

_____

8. We've updated this data to *incorporate* last quarter's *figures*.

_____

9. With her *impeccable* record, I don't *foresee* Reyna facing too many hiring *obstacles*.

_____

10. The *amended* recipe *necessitates* an *additional quantity* of cinnamon.

_____

Increasing reader interest and response rates through scannability

Watch + Learn

One of the most common concerns I hear when teaching live workshops is this: "My readers aren't responding to what I've asked for." Or, put another way: "I don't think my readers are even reading my requests fully."

If you're facing this issue with emails or other messages you send, I'll say this: Possibly, your readers just aren't *seeing* what you want them to do.

This doesn't mean you didn't say it or didn't explain it well. And it doesn't necessarily mean they're ignoring you either! It might simply mean that when they first opened your message, they didn't immediately see what to do… and then they got distracted and didn't follow up. Maybe they got pulled away and then never came back to the message.

While most of us try our best to explain everything we need to in a given message, this can actually end up working *against* us at times. The more information we provide, the less likely our readers are to see a specific piece of information.

When we provide easy-to-access, clear, concise, and even *visually easy* information, our readers will more likely "get it" about our message right away—before getting distracted. Even if they do get pulled away partway through our message, they would more likely have learned the crucial part before doing so if it were easily visible.

Let's put this to the test. Below, I'll offer similar information presented in two different ways: less scannable and more scannable. See which you'd rather read—and which you find easier to learn from. Note the different ways a reader can "see" information in the second version.

LESS SCANNABLE	MORE SCANNABLE
It is important that Management receive survey responses to our UX survey by the end of Q2. There are a few steps required to complete the survey. You must log in through the employee portal, submit your answers, and then follow it up with an email to your supervisor.	Please complete the required UX survey by the end of Q2. To complete your survey: 1. Log in <u>here</u>. 2. Answer all questions. 3. Click "Submit." 4. Wait for confirmation email. 5. Forward your confirmation to your supervisor.

Scannable information is simply easier to notice, take in, and even recall and respond to. If I'm reading the second example above, I learn all this information—just through visual cues—immediately:

- This message is directed at me.
- I'm going to have to do things.
- It looks like I have 5 steps to take.
- I have access to resources through a link.

Even before truly "reading" anything at all, then, I'm already aware I have to take action. That's huge! How many times have you written to someone, asked them to take action, and they simply haven't? How many times have you been told something along the lines of, "Oh! I didn't realize I had to *do* something!"?

The best time to use a bulleted list is typically when you find consistent types of information in a paragraph. For example, if you've listed multiple steps, multiple action items, multiple items, or multiple data points, you may be bullet-ready. Our goal is once again to help our reader find and use information quickly and easily—and without confusion. Pulling actions or other crucial points out of a paragraph where they could feel "hidden" from the reader can help.

Headings also help make our writing scannable. For example, when I'm emailing with a client about an upcoming workshop, I'll often use headings like "Proposed Curriculum" and "Scope and Costs" for different sections of my email. By doing so, the information not only becomes more visible, but readers can skip to the parts they find most relevant.

Most workplace readers skim the messages they receive to find the parts that apply to them specifically. We can help them do this by using headings that point them in the right direction. We want them to think, "This part's for me!" when they get to the pertinent heading. Therefore, we should write headings that help separate content into different areas of need when we can.

Let's look at an example. We'll do a sort of step-by-step Before and After. Based on the information included in the paragraph below, how would you:

- Use 2-3 internal headings to sort and announce content?
- Create bulleted lists out of specific paragraph content?

BEFORE

It is of critical importance that all machine operators consider the required safety protocols when using equipment on the floor. You are also required to keep your work area clean and prevent hazards by reducing clutter and mess. The safety protocols require that you use safety goggles when operating any equipment. You should also avoid overloading the machine. There are weight and volume limits listed on the side of the machine.

While the **BEFORE** paragraph strives to increase safety and reduce hazards, that's only going to become a reality if it gets read. And yet, some of the most crucial elements are nearly hidden in the paragraph. For instance, wearing goggles.

By using headings and bullets to organize the information, we make it more visually scannable for our readers. This in turn increases compliance and understanding. Here's how I might try dividing up the topics in the above paragraph, and integrating some bulleted lists.

AFTER

Please follow safety and clean-up protocols when using the machinery.

Safety Requirements

When using the machine, make sure you:

- Wear safety goggles
- Follow weight and volume limitations, as listed on the side of the machine

Clean-up Requirements

After using the machine, please make sure the area is free of:

- Mess and clutter
- Spare or used parts

Using Headings and Bullets to Make Your Writing Scannable

Create a heading and set of bullets to represent some of the information shared in each practice problem.

1. Our Customer Service team will now offer a variety of types of appointments to help meet everyone's needs. You can now make an appointment to discuss your application in person, through video chat, or on the phone. Once you've discussed your application with one of our representatives, you will then need to submit all required paperwork through our online portal, as well as upload two letters of recommendation.

_____

_____

_____

_____

_____

2. We are collecting proposals as we need a new vendor to provide maintenance services in three of our locations: Downtown, Uptown, and the Southern Extension. The selected vendor will be hired to perform services like landscape maintenance, indoor janitorial services, and upkeep inventory of supplies.

_____

_____

_____

_____

_____

3. A new veterinary clinic has opened in the Northern Heights, and they serve animals like dogs, cats, birds, and even horses. You have a few options for making appointments: call them up, use the appointment calendar on the website, or send them an email.

_____

_____

_____

_____

_____

Managing your reader's focus with intentional use of active/passive voice

We can also manage our reader's focus intentionally by using active or passive voice in specific situations. By choosing active or passive voice with purpose, we can highlight different ideas in our writing and steer our reader's attention. This helps us cut through the noise and make sure our readers see what we consider most important. We can use this ability to impact our reader's perceptions about what matters and even to urge them to take action.

Watch + Learn

The first words of a sentence tend to get extra attention from a reader and can even help set a tone for the whole sentence. Active and passive voice specifically impact word order. Therefore, just as writing with scannability can help us make our main points more visible, active and passive voice can help us bring important concepts to the front of a sentence. This makes those concepts easier to see, find, remember, and act on.

In the sentences below, notice the way your attention changes according to what's presented first. You'll see an (A) or (P) at the end of each sentence, clarifying whether it's active or passive.

Example A: *Interviews and Hiring*

Devon led the committee, which interviewed eight candidates. (A)

Eight candidates were interviewed by the committee, which was led by Devon. (P)

The committee interviewed eight candidates. (A)

Example B: *Annual Report Covering Data and Research*

We analyzed data from the last three research studies in our annual report. (A)

The data is discussed in the annual report. (P)

The annual report includes data analysis from three research studies. (A)

Three research studies are analyzed in this year's annual report. (P)

Example C: *Materials and Manufacturing*

Shut the fume hood when using this machine. (A)

The fume hood should always be shut when using this machine. (P)

This machine's fume hood needs to be shut during use. (A)

Keep the fume hood closed when using this machine. (A)

The above examples show us how active and passive voice can be used to manage our reader's attention. For example, in Example A, I might choose the passive example so I can highlight the candidates themselves. Or I could choose passive for Example B, to highlight the data; or in Example C, to highlight the fume hood.

In fact, I just used this trick in the previous paragraph! The first sentence includes passive language around "active and passive voice can be used to…." To state this in active voice, I would've needed to write "We can use active and passive voice to…." However, I chose passive so I could present the concept of "active and passive voice" first—as a tool available for our use.

You may have also noticed the way most of the passive sentences in the previous examples are longer than the active ones. This is typical: using passive voice usually makes us use more words—and more "fluff words" specifically. For this reason, try to use active voice as often as possible, and as your central writing voice. But bring in passive when you have a specific reason to do so.

In the next revision exercise, try shifting between active and passive voice to highlight different ideas. If helpful, feel free to consult the quick review below, which explains how to use active and passive voice.

How to Write in Active or Passive Voice

ACTIVE VOICE	PASSIVE VOICE
Who + What	**What + Who**
The committee interviewed five candidates.	Five candidates were interviewed by the committee.
Yogamatic offers this introductory yoga class.	This introductory yoga class is offered by Yogamatic.

 Cutting through the Noise with Intentional Active and Passive Voice
Revise the sentences below to bring focus to the suggested topic. In some cases, you'll change from active to passive; in others, you'll shift from passive to active.

BEFORE: Erin took the last bagel from the conference room. (A)

AFTER: *(Shift focus to bagels):* The last bagel was taken from the conference room. (P) or The bagels in the conference room have been finished. (P)

BEFORE: To rent this space, we require proof of income. (A)

AFTER: *(Shift focus to the requirement):* Proof of income is required to rent this space. (P)

Shift from active to passive to manage reader focus:

1. We just added breakfast sandwiches to the menu. (A) *(Shift focus to sandwiches.)*

   _____

2. Management added the whole county to your sales territory. (A) *(Shift focus to the county.)*

   _____

3. The lead designer incorporated your ideas into the third sample. (A) *(Shift focus to the ideas.)*

   _____

4. Our newest employee sold more cars last week than anyone else. (A) *(Shift focus to the cars.)*

   _____

5. Human Resources has requested your emergency contact information. (A) *(Shift focus to the contact information.)*

   _____

Shift from passive to active to manage reader focus and write more concisely:
(Note: Your sentences should get shorter this time around!)

6. All the students were taught by the visiting lecturer. (P) *(Shift focus to the lecturer.)*

_____

7. Our electrical wiring has been updated by a locally-owned company. (P) *(Shift focus to the company.)*

_____

8. A new scheduling assistant has been added by IT to all computers on the network. (P) *(Shift focus to IT.)*

_____

9. All the plants in the lobby are cared for by volunteers. (P) *(Shift focus to volunteers.)*

_____

10. We were asked by Management to participate in this survey. (P) *(Shift focus to Management.)*

_____

Clarifying your message by preventing detail overload

We've looked at a few ways to make our messages stand out so far: using familiar words, making our central points easily visible, and steering our reader's attention.

Watch + Learn

But helping our readers find our central message doesn't stop there—especially in complex situations with lots of details to consider. We can also use strategies to manage the amount of detail in our message, thereby ensuring the important parts get seen, read, and responded to. While we do want to avoid under-informing our readers, "detail overwhelm" doesn't necessarily help anyone either.

By managing our level of detail, and simply *reducing* the amount of text we ask our readers to take on, we can usually get closer to meeting our writing goals. On the other hand, though, what if we take out important details the reader needs? We might end up getting lots of phone calls or written messages, asking for clarification.

To avoid over-informing and under-informing, consider using the Now/Later/Never writing strategy for managing details. Here's how it works:

When you're writing, consider the many points you want to make. Then, do an honest assessment: When does your reader need each piece of information? Typically, they don't need *everything* we have to share right away. Instead, they might need some of the details later, at a later step, or when they're in a different situation.

For me, a classic over-explainer, I have to consider a third possibility: Maybe my reader doesn't need a particular piece of information either now or later. Maybe, in some cases, they just need that information "never."

Let's put this into action. Below, you'll find an example analysis using the Now/Later/Never process. And then one for you to try.

NOW/LATER/NEVER EXAMPLE ANALYSIS

Situation: Emailing a supervisor to suggest new products to sell at a toy store.

now	Which products you want to add
now	Whether new inventory is needed right now
later	Why you like these products
now	Market research supporting this idea
never	Studies into childhood toy preferences
never	Why you think they're a good addition
later	Which companies the products were made by
now	Your proposed timeline
now	Costs of the inventory
now	Projected sales and profits

There aren't really "right answers" to an analysis like this. The answer will vary, according to what you think your reader will respond to most. Here's a quick overview of how I like to decide whether to share something now, later, or never:

Now: Information that will impact Step 1 of the decision-making process

Later: Anything that will also help—but after Step 1

Never: Anything I'd like to include because I find it interesting, or other information that's relevant but not required for making a decision

Managing Detail with the Now/Later/Never Process

Write "Now," "Later," or "Never" next to each of the following items. Then, use the space at the bottom to reflect on your reasoning.

Situation: Emailing your supervisor to support hiring a specific speaker for an upcoming internal conference.

_____ Why you like the speaker you're suggesting

_____ What topics they cover

_____ Their speaking fee and potential travel costs

_____ How their topic is relevant to your audience

_____ Who they can provide as a reference

_____ Where your supervisor can see a video of them speaking

_____ How this speaker will be relevant to different departments

_____ This speaker's history, background, and education

_____ Other speakers being considered

_____ What you find important in a speaker

Reflection: How did you make your decisions? How did you think this through? Record your notes so you can look back on them next time you're faced with a similar decision.

_____

_____

_____

_____

_____

_____

_____

Key Takeaways & Action Items

You can use this page to record your most important insights, and keep track of the things you want to take action on. Reviewing and paraphrasing what you've learned will also help you remember and feel confident about what we've discussed and practiced.

Most impactful insights:

_____

_____

_____

Best strategies, tips, or tricks:

_____

_____

_____

Areas you'll apply these ideas (situations or types of documents/messages):

_____

One-sentence summary that captures the main point of this chapter:

_____

One word or phrase that captures the theme of this chapter: _____

"Before and After" Examples:

Before: _____

_____

After: _____

_____

Before: _____

_____

After: _____

_____

Making Your Point and Calling for Action

Jason, a vice president at a financial institution, emailed his organization's entire staff directory with some information about new workshops their learning department planned to hold.

"Sign up through this link by Friday!" the email offered. And when readers visited the link, they indeed found exactly what they needed: a way to register.

But Jason's recipients weren't registering.

"Did you include a call to action?" I asked Jason when he told me his troubles.

"Yes!" he said. "Exactly like you said to. I led with a command verb, and then I included a deadline and location—in this case, a link."

At first, I wasn't sure what to think. If he's offering a clear call to action, complete with the actual resource link, why wasn't anyone signing up? I had a new thought:

"Where did you put your call to action?" I asked.

"Well," Jason began, "I started by saying we have new classes to offer, and then I even gave the background and told them what each class would cover."

"What about the call to action though?" I prodded. "The link and everything…. Where was that?"

Jason paused and reflected a moment. "You know…" he began, making a thinking face. "I actually put it at the very end of the email."

A lot of the interactive writing we do for work includes sharing information, or making and fulfilling requests. Writers ask a question; readers answer it. Writers ask for information; readers provide it. Writers call for action, and readers follow through and get it done. Or at least that's what we hope they do.

Thoughts?

But more and more people are telling me in class lately, "I'm just not getting the responses." Their readers aren't following through on their requested actions. In some cases, writers aren't even sure if readers have opened their messages. "Did they even read it?" participants will ask, exasperated.

Based on our discussions of content overload and scannability, we know one possible reason readers may not be responding or following through: They may simply not be seeing the request or call for action.

This is not to say the writer hasn't provided it. You likely have experienced this before. You look at your email or other message, see your call for action right there, and hit "send." And yet: nothing.

We can increase response rates from our readers by taking special care with how (and when!) we provide our main point and call to action. And when we're emailing, we can get strategic with our subject line as well— using it to help ensure our readers see our point and call to action before they even open our message.

Whenever I receive an email, I'm wondering two things:

1. What's this for?
2. What do I have to do?

By immediately clarifying a main point and call to action in our written messages, we can answer these questions right away for our readers. In emailing situations specifically, we also benefit from using a specific kind of subject line.

Put together, we can use a simple 3-step process when we email to ensure our reader gets our point and their required action. The 3 steps of this process are:

1. Writing a **main point sentence (MPS)** that offers complete information
2. Providing a **call to action (CTA)** that tells what to do, when, and where
3. Previewing both through a **two-part subject line** (when emailing)

Here's an example of the beginning of an email that includes all three steps:

Brochure Draft: Edits Requested by Thursday 3/14

Hi Felipe,

Marketing is finalizing this year's brochure, and we'd like to gather everyone's feedback by Thursday, 3/14. Please send your edits on the attached draft using MSWord Track Changes.

In many cases, after writing these three steps, you may be done with your email. Readers know what's happening and they know what to do. If there was any chance of them getting confused, we've reduced that by leading with a subject line that previews both the MPS and CTA. By the time our reader opens the email, they already know what topic and type of action is coming.

This chapter, then, will help you:

- Write a clear and complete main point sentence
- Provide a clear, actionable call to action
- Create intentional two-part email subject lines

Using the 5 Ws to create a strong main point sentence (MPS)

Most of us have an accidental habit of either over-explaining or under-explaining. When we over-explain, our central points can become hidden from the reader. When we under-explain, a reader may be left unable to act because we haven't shared all the information they need to do so.

Creating an MPS that includes *who, what, when, where,* and *why* can help. This single sentence can become our main point. It's easier to find than explanations hidden in paragraphs. And it's complete as well: by learning all 5 Ws, a reader will typically know everything they need to know to understand and act.

Leading with an MPS can also help us get started with our writing. Sometimes, it's just tough to know how to begin a message. By noting the 5 Ws of your intended message, you can then combine these ideas into a sentence. And then? Wham! You've written your first line!

For example, I might create an MPS out of the following information:

Who: Caring County

What: holding a food drive

When: in December

Where: bins in the lobby

Why: to support our community

By putting these ideas into one solid sentence, we'd end up with: *Caring County invites you to support our community this December by donating food through our bins in the lobby.*

This MPS would then become the first sentence in an email, post, or other message.

Keep in mind: we have options for order. I could reorganize my sentence into one of the following versions by putting, for example, the why or the when in the front. I might do this if it's important to me to bring attention to something specific. Information at the front of a sentence often gets highlighted in the reader's mind. Therefore, it's worth leading with whatever you think matters most.

- *Starting in December,* Caring County will collect food items in the bins in the lobby to support our community.

- *To support our community,* Caring County welcomes food donations in December, through the bins in our lobby.

An important thing to notice about the last two examples: even though we started with when or why, by then saying "Caring County will collect" or "Caring County welcomes," we're still using a Who + What structure for the main part of our sentence. In this way, we can still write concisely, even when we find it crucial to lead with other information first.

Writing a Main Point Sentence (MPS) with the 5 Ws

Write an MPS for each of the topics/purposes below. Include as many of the 5 Ws as you believe your reader would need. In all cases, you'll include Who and What. In many cases, you'll also want to include When, Where, or Why. (It's ok to invent details for this exercise.)

TOPIC: There's a new policy on working from home and in the office.

MPS: Leadership will share the new hybrid work policy in an email next week.

1. Two departments want to hire interns.

   _____

2. Volleyball sign-ups are starting.

   _____

3. Let's get a speaker who specializes in generational cultures.

   _____

4. Management doesn't like the current flowchart.

   _____

5. Your team is sharing about a new virtual option for appointments.

   _____

6. There's a new policy that cell phones can't be used.

_____

7. Changes to the kitchen and lobby are coming soon.

_____

8. There's new storage in the clinic, including cabinets in each exam room.

_____

9. The south entrance is blocked because of construction.

_____

10. We are going to have a canned food drive.

_____

Now that we've provided a strong MPS, our readers know the situation. They may still, however, need to know what (if anything) *they* need to do in response. That's where our call to action (CTA) comes in.

Providing a clear Call to Action (CTA) to support reader responses and follow-up

A CTA lets readers know what action is required of them. It should also give them any crucial information they'll need to successfully take that action.

Watch + Learn

In some cases, your MPS and CTA may be the same statement. Some sentences cover both what's going on, and what the reader needs to do in response. For example, information like "Apply for a new position through [this link] by March 31 for best consideration," may cover everything that needs to be said.

In most situations, though, the MPS and CTA will be separate sentences that work together. They'll each answer one of your reader's central questions:

- The MPS answers the question, "What's this for?"

- The CTA answers the question, "What do I need to do?"

If you're making a request or assigning a task, the CTA is especially important. It's easy to ask someone to do something while accidentally leaving out crucial information. To provide a strong CTA that prepares readers to act, we need to include:

- A command verb: a verb in the "do this" form, like "edit," "provide," "reply," or "adjust"

- A deadline

- A location (may be physical or digital)

 Help Readers Know What to Do with a Strong Call to Action (CTA)
Revise the weaker CTA into a strong CTA that includes a command verb, deadline, and location (when relevant).

BEFORE: I'd like you to provide suggestions based on this research.

AFTER: Please provide research-based suggestions through [this link] by Friday.

1. We need copies of two forms of federal ID.

   _____

2. I want to know your thoughts on the menu I'm planning for the retreat.

   _____

3. Can you review this draft before I submit it on Friday?

   _____

4. I'd like you to contact all the new suppliers and share our new shipping requirements.

   _____

5. We need all operators on the manufacturing floor to follow this new protocol.

   _____

6. I'm not sure if this camera I'm looking at for vlogging is the best one. Thoughts?

   _____

7. I need to know how many members of the community you've contacted.

   _____

8. I would like your feedback on the translation I did in this chapter.

_____

9. I recommend we use the introduction from Draft C. Do you agree?

_____

10. By downloading the app, you can pay bills and check your balance anytime.

_____

By including an MPS and CTA in your first (and possibly only) paragraph, you make it very likely that your reader will know what's happening and what to do. By layering on one more strategy (in the case of emailing specifically), we can make it even more likely.

Providing a two-part email subject line to increase reader response rates

When emailing, we can preview our MPS and CTA for our readers. By previewing *both* the topic and action of our message, our readers already know a little about email before even opening it. This means they're less likely to misunderstand or ignore the message—and more likely to understand and act on it.

Watch + Learn

Subject lines need to be informative, but short. There's no room for fluff or words that don't add meaning. For that reason, I suggest dividing our two parts with a colon rather than with more words. Then, use 2-3 words on one side of the colon to describe the topic, and the same for the action on the other side. The formula looks like either of these:

- Topic: Action. For example, *New Supplier: Create Profile by 3/25*

- Action: Topic. For example, *Create Profile by 3/25: New Supplier*

In a best-case scenario, we can also use this process to help our reader schedule or even begin their required action. For instance, if I get an email with the subject line, "Food Drive: Donate Next Week," I already know to stop at the store and get canned goods before even opening the message itself.

Increasing Reader Responses with a Two-Part Email Subject Line
Write a two-part subject line you'd use for an email on the given topic.

BEFORE: I'd like your feedback on this brochure draft by Friday

AFTER: Brochure Draft: Feedback by Friday Requested

1. Can you give me the name and email of the person I need to contact in Accounting?

   _____

2. I need the measurements and drawings of the new site proposal by Monday.

   _____

3. Can you please attach your resume and send by Wednesday?

   _____

4. Update, we don't have a working refrigerator; you'll have to move your food.

   _____

5. What are the specs on the new parts Company A is manufacturing for us?

   _____

6. Make sure you write all your performance reviews by the end of the month.

   _____

7. Who's in charge of testing the water for chlorine levels?

   _____

8. I'd like to nominate Person B to serve on the Equity Board.

   _____

9. Can we chat? I would like to share some thoughts on yesterday's meeting.

   _____

10. This patient's prescription has changed but it's not reflected in the file; please fix.

    _____

CLEAR, ACTIONABLE EMAILS IN 3 STEPS

The above sections explained how to write an MPS, CTA, and intentional email subject line. To do this every day in your professional writing, just run through these three steps to get there.

Watch + Learn

1. Write an MPS that includes Who, What, When, Where, and Why

2. Write a CTA that includes a command verb, deadline, and location (if relevant)

3. Write a two-part subject line with [topic]: [action]

EXAMPLE

Goal of the Email: Please recommend a business book for our upcoming learning session; the book should include innovative ideas and be good for a group of new managers.

1. We are looking for recommendations for a business book for our next learning session with our new managers.

2. Please enter your suggestions through [this link].

3. Learning Session: Book Recommendations Requested

Key Takeaways & Action Items

You can use this page to record your most important insights, and keep track of the things you want to take action on. Reviewing and paraphrasing what you've learned will also help you remember and feel confident about what we've discussed and practiced.

Most impactful insights:

_____

_____

_____

Best strategies, tips, or tricks:

_____

_____

_____

Areas you'll apply these ideas (situations or types of documents/messages):

_____

One-sentence summary that captures the main point of this chapter:

_____

One word or phrase that captures the theme of this chapter: _____

"Before and After" Examples:

Before: _____

_____

After: _____

_____

Before: _____

_____

After: _____

_____

Chapter 5

Writing with Flow and Guiding Your Reader

Earlier in this workbook, we talked about the content overload we and our readers face each day. To help with this, we as writers can intentionally help our readers see the most important parts of our messages by "frontloading" meaning and making it scannable. By writing concisely in general, everything we write stands a better chance of getting noticed, read, and responded to.

But what about when we're writing longer documents and emails? What if there will be lots of scrolling involved? How can we help our readers distinguish the important and actionable items in multipage documents and emails so that they can take action?

To support readers with busy mental loads, we need to provide guidance and signals to guide them through longer communications. We can use intentional wording—and intentional design choices—to help readers know the following as they read:

- Why am I reading this particular section?
- How does it relate to other sections?
- Do I need to act on this part, or just know about it?
- What's the most important thing I need to know or do?

If we don't make questions like those above easy to answer, we run the risk of not meeting our writing goals. After all, meeting our writing goals often partially depends on our reader! If a reader doesn't find their required action, they likely won't do what we need done. If a deadline isn't easily spotted, it likely won't be met.

We have a few tools in this arsenal. Specifically, we can use the following strategies to ease the mental work required to read and quickly digest even longer emails and documents:

- ⊙ Create flow by ensuring one idea leads to the next so readers don't get lost or distracted
- ⊙ Guide readers with topic sentences that help them navigate the message or document
- ⊙ Use reader analysis to create an intentional order of ideas

Thoughts?

Creating a logical sense of flow for your reader with conceptual links

Take a look at the following three pairs of sentences. Read through each one quickly, without trying too hard. Try to resist going back to decipher things that don't automatically feel clear. Which is the easiest to read, digest, or even learn from?

Watch + Learn

Goes with 58-62

- ❑ **A.** Our committee proposes hiring the fourth candidate, who taught in multiple countries. We are unanimous in thinking she will be a good addition to our team.

- ❑ **B.** Our committee proposes hiring the fourth candidate, who taught in multiple countries. Based on this experience, she'll make a great addition to our team.

- ❑ **C.** Our committee proposes hiring the fourth candidate, who taught in multiple countries. More so than the other candidates, she'll make a great addition to our team.

To me, the information in (B) gets filed away in my mind the most easily. Below, I'll highlight the words that I think make this happen:

> Our committee proposes hiring the fourth candidate, who taught in multiple countries. *Based on this experience,* she'll make a great addition to our team.

The italicized words above (from option B) create a thread or link between the first and second sentences. This link keeps the reader's mind present and helps them transition from the first to the second sentence— without having the chance to get distracted or even lost. In a world of content overload, this ability to capture and retain reader attention can help our messages get read completely.

Let's try another. Again, take a look at the following three pairs of sentences. Check the one that feels—on a gut level—the easiest to read, digest, or even learn from.

- ❑ **A.** Our college campus needs to increase safety measures, especially in parking lots. We need to make the area more lit-up at night.

- ❑ **B.** Facilities wants to put additional lights in the parking lot to increase safety. Other college campuses have done this with great success.

- ❑ **C.** Facilities wants to put additional lights in the parking lot to increase safety. Safety measures like these have helped on other college campuses.

- ❑ **D.** The parking lots may be getting additional lights as a safety measure. This will help students on our campus be safer.

In this case, option C offers a link at the start of the second sentence, much like we saw from option B in the previous example. The italicized words below offer that link:

> Facilities wants to put additional lights in the parking lot to increase safety. *Safety measures like these* have helped on other college campuses.

We're not changing content with this strategy, and we're not even changing our words that much either. What we're changing is the word order—or, more importantly, the order of the concepts in our second sentence.

We can reorder our words so we open a new sentence with a conceptual link to the previous one. This way, our reader's mind stays with us. To do this, make sure you open the second sentence wherever your reader's mind would've been after reading the first.

Watch + Learn

Try revising the second sentence in the following sentence pairs. You'll want to ensure the second sentence begins on the same thought left in the reader's mind from the first.

Note: Don't worry about revising the first sentence. You can typically create flow by just altering the lead of the second sentence. However, feel free to revise both if you think of an even better way to structure the whole pair!

Increasing Flow with Sentence Links and Intentional Word Order

Revise the second sentence in each pair below. Make sure your revised second sentence begins with the concept left in the reader's mind from the end of the first sentence.

BEFORE: The committee recommends we release this product in Q3, not Q2. We will have more time to plan our marketing approach by releasing the product later.

AFTER: The committee recommends we release this product in Q3, not Q2. By releasing the product later, we will have more time to plan our marketing approach.

BEFORE: We recommend creating a flowchart for this procedure. Readers tend to complete the required steps more when they have a flowchart.

AFTER: We recommend creating a flowchart for this procedure. When they use a flowchart, readers are more likely to complete the required steps.

1. The new recycling policy asks us to sort our recyclables and use the new bins provided by management. This policy is different from last year's because we now have three bins instead of two: recycling, compost, and landfill waste.

   _____

2. We decided to rent the space next to the shop and expand our services in the coming year. We've always wanted a bigger shop.

   _____

3. The drafted work instructions don't address the perspectives of the user very well. It is harder to understand work instructions that are written from the view of management only.

   _____

4. I'd like to hire the first candidate because of her HR experience. She can better understand how to support our teams and complete back-end documentation because of this experience.

   _____

5. We've been asked by Operations to update this process. They always say we can streamline our work with these updates.

---

6. Please provide background information on the third candidate. I would like to know more about the education and experience of this person.

---

7. We require all applicants to submit two forms of ID and three references. You can use the application portal to upload this information.

---

8. The Chemistry and Biology departments will receive new equipment as part of this year's budget. These departments haven't had lab upgrades in a while.

---

9. The surgical team read this book to work on their internal communication. They want to reduce misunderstandings by discussing their communication styles.

---

10. The distributor will drop off new products to add to our inventory. It will be helpful to have new products to offer local customers once we have this inventory.

We can extend this strategy beyond two specific sentences to create flow on a larger scale. When writing longer paragraphs, documents, or messages, we can refer back to conceptual links throughout. Our goal? Keeping our reader's mind with us, and keeping them on track as we explain our thoughts.

In a longer document or message, I'll use my paragraphs' topic sentences to "call back" conceptual links. Topic sentences help our readers in a variety of ways. They can also increase flow. A topic sentence, the first sentence in a given paragraph, is another of our best tools for creating flow. Topic sentences also increase reader compliance because they help readers understand what they're reading, making it more likely they'll continue.

Using topic sentences to increase flow and guide your reader

Take a look at the following two brief paragraphs. As you read, take note of your reactions. Which paragraph left you without questions, without confusion? Which took you less time to read? Which was easier to understand?

Watch + Learn

- **Example A:** The new courses will help teams communicate more smoothly internally, as well as prepare our Customer Service reps to better assist our customer base through email and direct messaging. Ask your manager about enrolling in one of the new workshops during Q2. Leadership decided to add three new communication courses to our internal offerings.

- **Example B:** Leadership decided to add three new communication courses to our internal offerings. The new courses will help teams communicate more smoothly internally, as well as prepare our Customer Service reps to better assist our customer base through email and direct messaging. Ask your manager about enrolling in one of the new workshops during Q2.

While the paragraphs cover the same information, they present it differently. Example A gets right into the specifics and reasons—which can feel good in some ways, like front-loading meaning. Example B, though, helps the reader in another way: *by getting them situated.* After reading the first sentence in Example B, we know two important things:

- What the coming paragraph will cover (topic)
- Why we'd want to know that information (relevance)

Example B, then, provides what I'd call navigation for the reader. It says, "Hey, here's where you are, and here's why we're presenting this info." Therefore, this strategy also helps us hold our readers' attention by making things clear, easy, and logical for them. By sharing both the paragraph's topic and its relevance with our readers early, we increase the chances they'll both complete the reading and act on it afterwards.

That's the power of a topic sentence (TS). Readers need it, even in professional writing. And writers need it too: to encourage our readers to read, understand, digest, and use everything we've written.

It can feel like writing a TS is just for school writing. Many of us learned the dreaded "5-Paragraph Essay" and may have gotten some "drill-and-kill" on writing a TS. However, using a TS to start a paragraph is even more crucial in professional writing than in academic writing in some ways. People reading messages and documents at work are busy with many competing interests, so a TS can help them focus on what we've written.

If you're writing a multi-paragraph document or message, topic sentences also offer another opportunity: done right, a reader can read only the topic sentences of the document/message and get a full summary.

Readers are more likely to read the initial sentences of paragraphs than the sentences within. So, by ensuring all our paragraphs' first sentences preview their paragraphs well, we can create a mini summary as well.

Let's go back to the two goals of a topic sentence to figure out how to write strong topic sentences that can ultimately also serve as a summary:

- *Topic:* A good TS lets the reader know the topic or main point of the paragraph.
- *Relevance:* A good TS helps the reader realize why the information matters.

Sometimes, writers create a TS that only accomplishes the first of the above two goals. We might say what the paragraph covers, but not indicate why it matters. This may decrease the likelihood of our readers reading the whole paragraph. Helping them see why to read it can help.

The examples below help show the difference between a TS that establishes relevance, and one that doesn't. While the "Before" examples read like statements of fact or description, the "After" examples show us why to care.

BEFORE: There are many proposed updates to the bike path.

AFTER: The proposed bike path updates can also boost local businesses by connecting the main path to the shops.

BEFORE: It is important to have an emergency plan and share it with everyone in your household.

AFTER: Creating a plan can increase your family's potential safety in an emergency.

The examples above show that by addressing relevance in a TS, we can increase the impact of an entire paragraph. Sharing why something matters both increases the likelihood of a complete paragraph read and makes it easier to digest that paragraph.

The TS offers a "heads-up" into both the meaning and application of the paragraph's concept. By reading this before the paragraph, our reader is ready to learn, understand, and act. To help our reader navigate, then, we should provide some indication of the "Why does this matter?" as well as the "What are we discussing?" elements.

If you have trouble with any of the revisions, try asking yourself "So what?" after reading one of the practice problem sentences. This might inspire exactly what content is needed to make the sentence more meaningful.

Increasing Reader Interest by Establishing Relevance in Topic Sentences

Revise the sentences below to create a strong topic sentence that includes relevance.

BEFORE: There are different ways to get a work permit.

AFTER: Minors need a work permit to get a job, and can follow two easy steps to get started.

1. This space can be rented for events.

   _____

2. IT has a process that includes creating a Help Ticket.

   _____

3. It is a requirement that you update your user profile.

   _____

4. Music theory is taught at some universities, but not others.

   _____

5. When applying to study abroad, you can provide a narrative describing your prior education and experience.

   _____

6. It is a requirement for new job applicants to take a written assessment.

   _____

7. This decision may have impacts on our organizational culture.

   _____

8. When scheduling tree trimming or other services, we have an online calendar app.

   _____

9. Assessing levee safety near rivers may be part of an environmental engineer's job.

   _____

10. It has been decided that we will add more appetizers to the happy hour menu.

    _____

By creating topic sentences that lead into paragraphs' topics and importance, we can offer our readers not only information, but a window into what to do with it. If our TS does two jobs at once, we're also writing efficiently, concisely, and economically.

Part of the extra power of a TS comes from the ability to simply be physically seen. A TS stands out because it comes right after an indent or an extra space. Therefore, readers will more likely read a TS than another sentence in a document because it's simply easier to see! We can leverage this visual ability by writing in a way that's "skimmable" and "scannable."

Using reader analysis to create an intentional order of ideas

We want our ideas to flow in any writing that's more than one sentence. And when we hit the paragraph level, we can include a topic sentence to help guide reader understanding.

In longer documents, we can also help readers by creating an intentional order of ideas that reflects their interests and needs. We want our structure of ideas to feel logical on the reader's end. To ensure longer documents get read, then, it helps to use a combined approach:

- Order ideas according to reader interest/need when feasible.
- Make sure ideas are in a logical order or reflect a structural plan.

If I'm writing about extreme weather, for example, keeping my reader's geography in mind will help me make informed writing decisions about my order of ideas. If I want to cover tornados, hurricanes, wildfires, and floods, I might order these ideas differently, depending on my reader's location.

For example, if my reader is in Florida, USA, I might lead with hurricanes. But if I then revise that writing for a reader in British Columbia, Canada, I'd reorganize and lead with wildfires.

We can always create an intentional order with our reader in mind. Let's put this idea to the test. Below, you'll find two lists of the same topics. The order of these topics, though, should be based on potential reader needs and interests. See if your lists turn out similar, vastly different, or somewhere in between.

Ordering Ideas According to Reader Interest and Need

Choose a (different) reader for each list, and then enter 1, 2, 3, 4, 5, and 6 in the blank spaces to indicate the order of ideas you'd use for this reader. In both situations, imagine you're sharing an update about a new project.

Reader Options (Circle one): Human Resources employees, Accounting staff, leadership team, all hands, the public, engineers on your team

_____ timeline

_____ costs

_____ environmental impacts

_____ who's involved

_____ impacts on other departments

_____ impacts on the community

Reader Options (Circle one): Human Resources managers, Accounting staff, leadership team, all hands, the public, engineers on your team

_____ timeline

_____ costs

_____ environmental impacts

_____ who's involved

_____ impacts on other departments

_____ impacts on the community

In addition to ordering ideas based on reader interest and need, we can also ensure our ideas are presented according to an internal sense of logic. In some cases, you may not be able to gauge your reader's interests and will need another organizational plan. In other cases, you can order ideas according to your reader's needs, but may have so many ideas to share that they need an internally logical order within them as well.

Typically, we can order ideas based on one of the following organizational plans:

- *Chronology*: listing ideas in the order they naturally occur
- *Cause and effect*: describing a cause for multiple paragraphs then moving to effects
- *Problem and solution*: describing a problem for multiple paragraphs then moving to a proposed solution
- *Compare and contrast*: organizing thoughts according to similarities and differences of two topics
- *Steps in a process*: listing ideas in the order they need to occur
- *Intentional categories*: creating categories out of longer lists of topics

The idea behind intentional categories is this: Instead of listing 12 topics and asking our reader to work their way through all 12, we first categorize our ideas, and then present a smaller number of topics which are actually categories.

With the extreme weather example, for instance, I might want to cover all of the following topics: tornados, hurricanes, wildfires, floods, earthquakes, heatwaves, loss of animal habitats, and loss of human homes. That's eight ideas. My reader will have an easier time, though, if I categorize them first, therefore sharing fewer ideas at once.

Using the intentional categories approach, I might only offer my reader three ideas:

1. Extreme weather is happening (include tornados through heatwaves).
2. This is impacting animal habitats.
3. This is impacting human homes.

When we go back to the idea of content overload from Chapter 3, we can imagine our reader having an easier time working their way through what appears to be three ideas instead of eight.

 ## Ordering Ideas Based on a Logical Organizational Pattern

For each of the writing situations below, write down which organizational pattern you'd use, from the following list: chronology, cause/effect, problem/solution, compare/contrast, process steps, intentional categories. If you choose intentional categories, add a note about what kinds of categories you'd use.

1. A briefing on the environmental impacts of a new factory.

_____

2. An email about the positive and negative impacts of the latest schedule changes.

_____

3. An annual report about health in a particular community.

_____

4. An article about the different ways to help communities develop neighborhood gardens.

_____

5. An email about employee satisfaction survey responses from employees in Gen X, Millennial, and Gen Z groups.

_____

6. A proposal addressing the need for more housing in a particular area of town.

_____

7. Website copy explaining how to use the new employee information portal.

_____

8. A brochure for homeowners, advocating planting trees to reduce heat.

_____

9. Website copy helping people living in apartments grow vegetables in portable planter beds.

_____

10. An email to all staff, sharing upcoming nearby road closures and parking options during construction.

_____

Key Takeaways & Action Items

You can use this page to record your most important insights, and keep track of the things you want to take action on. Reviewing and paraphrasing what you've learned will also help you remember and feel confident about what we've discussed and practiced.

Most impactful insights:

_____

_____

_____

Best strategies, tips, or tricks:

_____

_____

_____

Areas you'll apply these ideas (situations or types of documents/messages):

_____

One-sentence summary that captures the main point of this chapter:

_____

One word or phrase that captures the theme of this chapter: _____

"Before and After" Examples:

Before: _____

_____

After: _____

_____

Before: _____

_____

After: _____

_____

6
Writing to Build Trust, Respect, and Belonging

I recently worked one-on-one with Margaret, a young woman who was in her second "career job" and loving it.

"I called my mom at lunch my second day," she told me. She'd literally phoned her mom from the office to tell her all about how she felt included and cared for.

Unfortunately, she hadn't been able to say the same about her first big job, the one she'd excitedly landed right out of college.

"I just had to get out of there," she told me repeatedly. Even though it had been her first professional job, she knew what she was experiencing wasn't right.

"They didn't care about us at all," she explained. "Not like my new job, where they totally care. I feel like I belong here."

"How do you know whether you're being cared about by leadership or not?" I asked her. "What did they do? What did they say?"

"It's all in the emails," she answered.

Wow. All that from just an email?

In Margaret's first job—the one she'd left as soon as she could find another—leadership's monthly all-hands emails were all about what leadership had accomplished. She read sentences that started like, "Our CTO presented for…" or "Last year's figures have allowed us to …"

In her second job, she also received all-hands emails. But these set a very different culture. Suddenly, she and her colleagues were getting seen. She now read sentences that began with "Our IT team competed in…" or "Maya from IT encouraged us to adapt our strategy to…"

Who was getting the credit now? The people!

Thoughts?

When we write to people in emails or texts, we have a great opportunity to impact our relationship with them. We can also impact their perceptions of whatever we're writing about—and of us. By choosing our words intentionally, we can build trust, convey respect, and create a sense of belonging and community.

To accomplish these relational goals, we can:

- shift our reader's focus with intentional word choice
- write with other-focus
- share the spotlight with intention
- create togetherness with collective actions
- use active or passive voice to purposefully impact what matters

Managing our reader's focus with intentional word choice

You can easily increase or reduce the amount of attention, focus, credit, or blame someone receives through intentional word choice. By leveraging the Who + What sentence structure, and then choosing your Who with intention, you can highlight whoever you want or need to.

Goes with 23-26

Here's an example. Imagine you lead a committee that awards scholarships to first-generation college students. When you write about the process—and the winning students—you have options about whom to highlight. By highlighting someone specifically in your sentence, you increase the likelihood they'll get the credit for what's been accomplished.

By adjusting our Who with intention, we get options like:

A. *We* awarded 25 scholarships last year.

B. *Our team* awarded 25 scholarships last year.

C. *Liliana's team* awarded 25 scholarships last year.

D. *The Outreach Department* awarded 25 scholarships last year.

E. *25 students* received scholarships from us last year.

F. *25 students* earned scholarships from us last year.

In examples A-D above, we can see some of the different ways to credit the employees who made this happen. Or, as in E-F, we can credit the students. Examples E-F also illustrate the power of combining an intentional Who with a very intentional What. In F, not only have the students been empowered by coming first in the sentence, they're also credited with doing the actual work. They've "earned" scholarships themselves, not just "received" them.

Shifting Attention with Intentional Word Choice

Revise the sentences below to shift focus to the assigned person or group.

BEFORE: Management welcomes all employees to the retreat. (goal = shift focus to employees)

AFTER: You are invited to this year's retreat.

Shift attention to employees:

1. We invite all personnel to participate in shaping next year's retreat.

   _____

2. Leadership is interested in your thoughts about next year's retreat.

   _____

3. We've decided to get everyone's input before this year's retreat.

   _____

Shift power to the applicant:

4. We need you to provide two forms of government identification.

   _____

5. We still haven't received confirmation from one of your references.

   _____

6. It is a requirement that you provide a one-page bio.

   _____

Shift credit/responsibility from one person to the group:

7. I'm proud to say the record for sales in one weekend has been beat!

   _____

8. After you attend the session, please provide me with feedback through this link.

   _____

9. My Quality Assurance team reported only two errors last quarter.

   _____

We can intentionally alter power dynamics, increase belonging and recognition, and impact our teams directly, all through word choice and arrangement. How's that for strategic!? This workbook's introduction opened with the concept of increasing other-focus and reducing the self-focus we've often learned to write with. In this chapter, we've seen a few ways to focus on and empower others, and to encourage our readers to do the same. Let's look at some other strategies to achieve this relational goal in our writing.

Writing with other-focus to build community and team belonging

In many of my live workshops, I share a truth about writing. It seems obvious, but often, we haven't fully realized its implications:

If you're not journaling or note-taking, you're not writing for you.

That's right: If you're writing for work, or for daily life requirements, your writing probably exists solely for someone else. If you also write for fun, that's for you. But the writing we create to be used by others should be oriented to their needs and style when possible.

We don't always think about this simple truth, but reflecting on it can be empowering. While we might worry about our own writing style and mistakes when we're writing, whatever we're producing when we write for work doesn't actually exist for us. It exists for others.

Think about it: If I'm the one writing, it stands to reason that I already know the information. That means the information I'm providing is for someone other than me.

Though it's not on purpose, many of us write with self-focus. We're naturally worried about our own needs and also about our own writing struggles and successes. We can get a little bit "in our heads" when writing.

Successful professional writing, however, is other-focused. It's made for others, after all. It takes into account the needs of the reader, as well as the impacts of tone and interpretation. In short, good writing recognizes the "interactive" element of writing and reading.

Supervisors can leverage this truth about the impacts of writing by using intentional writing as a tool for effective leadership and management. Intentional language can help leaders inspire, direct, redirect, motivate, or build community.

By writing with intention, leaders and managers can also use their writing to create specific perceptions and behaviors among their teams. Intentional writing can help us motivate, include, direct, or redirect a reader, for example.

Watch + Learn

Team members can similarly use these other-focus techniques—with purpose and intention—to impact their professional relationships and career growth. Intentional language can help all of us manage not only our messages but also the way we connect with others in our professional and personal lives.

Part of writing with other-focus means reducing the amount of I, my, mine, and me in our writing—and increasing the amount of we, us, our, and team. Other-focus in writing also means we consider our reader's needs and preferences—and write to intentionally build respect and community.

 ## Writing with Other-Focus to Build Community and Team Belonging

Revise the sentences below to take the focus off the writer, and shift the focus to others—either the reader, the group or team, or others referred to in the writing.

BEFORE: My team achieved growth even during an economic downturn.

AFTER: Our team achieved growth even during an economic downturn.

1. I have still not heard from any of you about volunteering to facilitate the next meeting.

   _____

2. I'm interested in learning more about your ideas in Sales and bringing them back to my team in Marketing.

   _____

3. Can you let me know how early you will each arrive at the event?

   _____

4. I'm so proud of my team.

   _____

5. Would you like to attend the session with the others?

   _____

6. This draft still needs a lot of edits, and you should ask Priya and Dave for help.

   _____

7. The data my team reported hasn't changed since last quarter.

   _____

8. Each person in this department makes important contributions every day.

_____

9. I would like feedback from each of you on the proposed spring menu.

_____

10. I've asked IT to load this new AI product on each computer on the network.

_____

Sharing the spotlight helps us build belonging and give credit

We can also give credit and attention to others and their work more specifically by intentionally rotating who gets spotlighted in our sentences. Instead of focusing on writer contributions, we can shine the spotlight on the contributions of other individuals specifically.

Just as we highlighted group efforts in the previous exercise, we can also intentionally shift the spotlight to individuals. Leaders can highlight the contributions of specific people to meet management goals like:

Watch + Learn

- encouraging a less participatory team member
- giving credit to someone whose ideas have been overlooked
- connecting team members intentionally
- conveying a sense of respect for the entire team's efforts

To achieve management goals through our writing, we have a few options. Our main goal is to make a sentence "about" whoever we're sharing the spotlight with. Try rearranging word order, leading with someone's name, or otherwise bringing attention to someone's accomplishments. You can also add powerful verbs to show the strong actions of those you write about.

Sharing the Spotlight to Build Belonging and Give Credit

Revise the sentences below to intentionally share the spotlight. Shift the focus from the writer or department, and shine the spotlight on someone else in the sentence. Feel free to add a name or other words you need to create the most impactful sentence.

BEFORE: This decision was informed by our IT team.

AFTER: Sasha from IT guided our decision.

1. The Marketing department had another amazing year!

   _____

2. My Quality Assurance team hit a new low of 4% errors this month.

   _____

3. Human Resources is offering free registration for all staff to join our annual summer Nutrition Program.

   _____

4. Please follow the instructions provided by management so you can have the best experience with this procedure.

   _____

5. I've assigned each of you a specific part of the project; when everyone does their part, we'll have a strong outcome.

   _____

6. We have included all of this year's data in our latest report.

   _____

7. We asked Marketing to create a flier, and we're happy with the results.

   _____

8. Each month, we rotate who facilitates our team meetings, and this month is no different.

   _____

9. I'm interested in learning more about your ideas and bringing them back to my team.

   _____

10. Management has asked for two representatives from my team.

_____

Using collective actions to increase a sense of togetherness

Part of being on a team means getting things done through collaboration. We can show people accomplishing things together by using collective verbs—actions people do together. Writing to show collective team or group actions helps create a sense of community and belonging.

By showing people accomplishing things together, we can convey a natural sense of belonging and community. We can use "we," "our team," or team members' names as our Who, and then add a verb the group does together right after our Who.

For example, instead of separating a leader from their team, we can create a sense of togetherness with intentional verb choice. Instead of, for instance, "I need Marketing to submit metrics and Outreach to post your timeline for next quarter," we could revise with a _collective verb_, like:

- Let's have Marketing and Outreach _share_ relevant metrics and timelines.
- _We look forward to learning_ metrics from Marketing and timelines from Outreach.

Using Collective Actions to Increase Togetherness
Revise each sentence to use a verb that everyone does together.

BEFORE: So many of us were included in this project.

AFTER: Together, we _completed_ this project.

BEFORE: I have to assign this task to three of you.

AFTER: Can you three _tackle_ this problem?

1. Management has asked me to distribute this survey to each person on the team.

_____

2. It looks like another safety training will be required.

_____

3. We can get this done faster if some of you draft the brochure and others edit.

_____

4. New equipment is needed in the kitchen for both prep staff and clean-up staff.

_____

5. It would be great if whenever you all write to the executives, you keep it brief.

_____

6. It's great to see the success of the department's latest new product this year.

_____

7. The reception area might be more welcoming with plants and more color on the walls.

_____

8. I'm glad we had volunteers covering snacks for each of the games last season.

_____

9. Those of you working to sign up new clients are all invited to the retreat.

_____

10. I still haven't received updates from many of you on this team.

_____

Using active or passive voice can impact meaning, tone, and who matters

In Chapter 4, we discussed choosing active or passive voice on purpose to impact meaning and reader perceptions. We can also leverage these impacts to intentionally build respect and belonging through language.

By choosing one voice or the other, we can bring attention to people we intentionally want to include. We can also steer our reader's focus, and therefore, their perception—impacting who or what feels most important in a given sentence.

Let's revisit that ability to use active or passive voice with intention—but apply it more specifically to community-building and team morale. In the exercises below, try using our active and passive voice knowledge to intentionally shift the reader's focus.

Watch + Learn

Goes with 41-45

Using Active or Passive Voice to Increase Respect and Belonging

Revise each sentence to shift the focus from the writer or manager to the group or product/outcome. Consider revising from active to passive, or passive to active, to make this happen. (The sentences below are labeled (A) when in active voice and (P) when in passive voice.) You can also bring more focus to the group or product/outcome by just moving the team members or product/outcome to the front of the sentence.

BEFORE: I assigned each of you a part of this project. (A)

AFTER: Everyone will be assigned a part of this project. (P)

BEFORE: The meeting was facilitated smoothly last week. (P)

AFTER: Jayda facilitated our meeting smoothly last week. (A)

1. I liked the drafts Breanna submitted last week. (A)

_____

2. It has been announced that we will close early Friday. (P)

_____

3. Management chose the option Dylan presented. (A)

_____

4. The doors are locked by Security at 7 p.m. (P)

_____

5. Our team, led by Leslie's efforts, created a new recipe. (A)

_____

6. The shipment from Bagger Bagels has been ordered by Derek. (P)

_____

7. The new logo, which was created by Angelica, is ready. (A)

_____

8. Our subscription to the video chat platform has been renewed by Bryan. (P)

_____

9. I am proud of the progress Myrriah has made this year. (A)

_____

10. A new equipment update request has been submitted by Jonah. (P)

_____

Key Takeaways & Action Items

You can use this page to record your most important insights, and keep track of the things you want to take action on. Reviewing and paraphrasing what you've learned will also help you remember and feel confident about what we've discussed and practiced.

Most impactful insights:

_____

_____

_____

Best strategies, tips, or tricks:

_____

_____

_____

Areas you'll apply these ideas (situations or types of documents/messages):

_____

One-sentence summary that captures the main point of this chapter:

_____

One word or phrase that captures the theme of this chapter: _____

"Before and After" Examples:

Before: _____

_____

After: _____

_____

Before: _____

_____

After: _____

_____

Chapter
7

Targeting Your Message by Thinking about Your Reader

Manuel had only been a supervisor for two weeks when his own supervisor asked him to email her a "quick update" on his team's progress with a particular project.

"I was so excited!" Manuel shared in class. As a new leader, he was super proud of his team and couldn't wait to share about their work.

But later, as we discussed meeting readers' needs and preferences, Manuel came to feel his "brief update" had been anything but. As we talked about guiding one's reader, and making our writing work for them, Manuel had a realization:

"I have a confession," he shared, raising his hand.

We all turned to look.

"Is it about your 'update'?" I asked, teasingly. Manuel had just shared the truth about his "update"—that it had come to six paragraphs total—and I'd been getting curious.

"Indeed it is," he confessed, smiling.

"What have you realized?" I asked. We all listened up.

"You know, my boss? The one I sent my 6-paragraph update to?" he began.

"Yeah…?" many of us replied, waiting.

"Well I was just thinking about her and you know what: She's a bottom-line person. She's the exact opposite of someone who wants six paragraphs of updates."

Writing with other-focus, as discussed in Chapter 6, includes making specific writing decisions to target our reader. By making our written product as relevant to them as possible, we increase the chance of achieving our message's goal.

Thoughts?

We can also better target our reader by using communication styles that work for them. If we know our reader prefers a deep level of detail, we'd include that in a message. If they prefer formal communication, we might write more formally when contacting that reader specifically.

This chapter will expand on the concept of writing for others by looking at ways to understand our readers. We'll look at our readers from two vantage points: the reader as an individual, and the reader as a member of various groups. Both individuals and groups can have their own communication preferences, so we want to consider both when analyzing our reader to target our message.

Specifically, we'll consider:

- ⊙ Individual Communication Preferences
  - Personal reader preferences
  - Preferences based on a reader's role or position
- ⊙ Group Communication Preferences
  - Industry, career, or subject area background
  - Regional cultures
  - Generational cultures

Analyzing specific reader needs and communication preferences

Watch + Learn

We saw from Manuel's experience how readers can be quite specific in the way they like to receive information. Some of us want lots of detail; others want a little. Some readers are more easily persuaded when shown facts and figures; others respond to stories and sharing personal experiences.

As writers, we'll more often achieve the goal of our writing when we consider what works best for our readers. Most readers have communication preferences—whether they know it or not. By writing with these preferences in mind, we can more often target our message to ensure it works for our reader and helps us achieve our goals.

Specifically, it helps to consider some or all of the following when analyzing an individual reader:

- Their preferred level of formality
- How much detail they like to receive
- What's persuasive for them
- How their own goals, responsibilities, or constraints could impact the way they interpret your message

Analyzing Your Reader and Their Communication Preferences

Think about someone you write to often, and consider their potential communication preferences.

Name or Role/Position of Reader

_____

Your Relationship with this Reader

_____

CHECK ALL THAT APPLY

My reader typically prefers:

- ❑ Short messages
- ❑ Long messages
- ❑ A lot of detail
- ❑ Just the bottom line or main point
- ❑ A formal tone
- ❑ A more casual or informal tone
- ❑ Paragraphs with description
- ❑ Bulleted lists when feasible

CHECK ALL THAT APPLY

My reader is more likely to be persuaded or impacted by:

- ❑ Facts and figures
- ❑ Stories or sharing personal experience

Reader preferences can also be impacted by their role or position

The needs and preferences of our readers can also vary based on what they're required to do in their role. Therefore, even if you don't know your reader well, it's worth thinking about any communication preferences their role might create. We can also consider whether people with similar positions tend to have a certain communication preference.

For example, in most of my live sessions, participants say their writing gets briefer the "higher up" the ladder their reader. Readers at the executive level, for example, are said to prefer bottom-line information in most messages because they're required to make so many decisions per day.

Other participants share the way they adjust the actual content of their writing based on a reader's role or position—even when they don't know them. "People in Accounting typically need to know X and Y," they'll say. Or, "I'm in Design and I know other Designers prefer to hear information like A and B.

Of course, not all readers with similar roles will have the same communication expectations. But, it's worth thinking through the requirements (and constraints) of our reader's role when we think that can help inform our writing decisions.

Considering the Impact of Role/Position on Your Reader's Needs and Preferences

Think about someone you write to often, and consider whether any of their communication preferences might be impacted by their role. Or, try analyzing a reader you know less about—and see if considering their role helps you make any "educated guesses" about their potential communication preferences.

Role/Position of Reader	General Responsibilities of this Reader (Brief Summary)

CHECK ALL THAT APPLY

A reader with this role might often need to know:

- ☐ Who is responsible for something
- ☐ Deadlines and timelines
- ☐ Data and research
- ☐ Anecdotes and examples
- ☐ Background and context
- ☐ Who else is involved
- ☐ How others might be affected by the topic or decision at hand

CHECK ALL THAT APPLY

My reader might be constrained by:

- ☐ A busy schedule
- ☐ Lack of funding
- ☐ Lack of authority to make a specific decision
- ☐ People resources: labor, hours, etc.
- ☐ Conflicting priorities from other stakeholders

Understanding our readers' needs and situations can help us pinpoint our communication to be as relevant as possible to a given reader. To broaden our analysis, we can also consider the cultural groups our readers have participated in. Cultures have norms and expectations for communicating, so can impact the way a reader responds to a message.

For our purposes, we'll focus on three kinds of cultures: industry, generational, and regional. Although each culture has its norms, we should also remember that individuals also have their own specific perspectives, which may vary from the more general cultures they're part of. For example, I'm in Generation X, but I appreciate using many of the communication styles I hear associated with Millennials.

While writing to individuals who are part of groups, we want to first consider the individual reader—but then check to see if we need to adapt our communication based on any of their potential cultural norms.

Considering culture can help us build trust while communicating

All of us belong to several types of cultures, which can impact our norms, beliefs, expectations, and assumptions about communication. Based on discussions in the classroom, I think the most impactful aspects of culture, when it comes to communication, are:

- Industry culture
- Generational culture
- Regional or national culture

Watch + Learn

Goes with 89-93

All three of the above aspects of our cultures come with their own opinions about communication. I've worked in industries that expect either formal communication or casual messages. I've taught in countries where active voice feels aggressive and potentially rude—not clear and helpful the way it might in the United States, for example. Finally, I expect most of us have experienced communication breakdowns when writing across generations.

Whether we're emailing, posting, texting, or creating documents, the cultural preferences and expectations of our readers matter. While we can't know everything about what our readers expect, or what they find surprising, we can reflect on a few specifics before communicating across cultures—to increase our chances of success.

Level of Directness: Some cultures prefer to communicate very directly while others are more indirect.

> **More direct** (*often appreciated in the United States and Western Europe*):
> I'd like you to choose a different designer.

> **Less direct** (*often appreciated in East and Southeast Asia*):
> I've observed some differences between the designer's style and our team's needs.

Level of Formality: In some settings, communicating with a more formal approach to punctuation and word choice makes sense. In others, sounding very formal could create distance between the writer and reader.

> **More formal** (*often appreciated in industries like law, medicine, academia*):
> We request your presence at this year's holiday celebration Thursday after business hours.

> **Less formal** (*often appreciated in smaller businesses, K-12 education, or those serving the community*):
> Please join our holiday party Thursday after work.

Level of Hierarchy: Some cultures put a greater emphasis on titles and create a larger separation between "levels" of employees than others. In some cultures, people across levels (or across the "hierarchy" or organizational structure) communicate as equals. In others, more formal communication can be expected by leadership or management.

> **More hierarchical:**
> It has been requested by Management that you provide feedback.

> **Less hierarchical:**
> Please share your feedback [here].

Writing to Respect Different Cultural Preferences and Expectations

Alter the tone of each sentence, according to the suggestion, through intentional word choice.

BEFORE: I would like to request we have a talk in my office later today. (Make more informal)

AFTER: Can you join me in my office to chat later today?

Make more formal:

1. What's your opinion on this?

   _____

2. Am I too late to apply for this job?

   _____

3. I don't know if I can afford this service; how much monthly?

   _____

Make more informal:

4. It is at my request that the director offers the session on an alternate date.

   _____

5. After analyzing the third draft, I must concur with Katrina.

   _____

6. If it is feasible, we would appreciate the honor of a follow-up session.

   _____

Make more direct:

7. I'm not sure if this idea would fit with the third requirement.

   _____

8. We would like to reconsider whether or not the obligations have been met.

   _____

9. If you have time, I would appreciate some help during third shift.

Make more indirect:

10. I don't agree with the director at all.

_____

11. This schedule is bad for me this week.

_____

12. You need to revise this draft and get some help on the grammar.

_____

Make more hierarchical:

13. I'd love to be a part of this effort if you'll have me!

_____

14. We invited anyone who wanted to join and a few directors did.

_____

15. I've only been here two years, but I think these ideas will help you see things a new way.

_____

Make less hierarchical:

16. Employees on your floor are required by management to watch this safety briefing.

_____

17. Her staff is still working away on that project.

_____

18. We invited everyone—from first floor inventory to the executives on the 16th floor.

_____

Key Takeaways & Action Items

You can use this page to record your most important insights, and keep track of the things you want to take action on. Reviewing and paraphrasing what you've learned will also help you remember and feel confident about what we've discussed and practiced.

Most impactful insights:

_____

_____

_____

Best strategies, tips, or tricks:

_____

_____

_____

Areas you'll apply these ideas (situations or types of documents/messages):

_____

One-sentence summary that captures the main point of this chapter:

_____

One word or phrase that captures the theme of this chapter: _____

"Before and After" Examples:

Before: _____

_____

After: _____

_____

Before: _____

_____

After: _____

_____

Chapter
8
Using Strategic Writing as a Management Tool

When I taught college writing classes, I'd read and comment on a lot of papers. When wordsmithing comments on students' papers, I had a general rule that I'd use *you/your* when the student had made excellent writing choices. However, when they'd missed the goal in some way, I would shift the focus of my comments from them as a writer to the paragraph or page being discussed.

Thoughts?

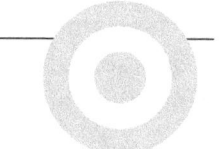

"You supported your point with such solid evidence on page 3," I might write.

But if they didn't, I would *not* write "You failed to support your point with evidence on page 3." I knew, from being human myself, that this wouldn't leave my students feeling super motivated or open to discussing their work.

Instead, I'd write something like, "Page 3 needs more evidence."

More often than not, this approach would lead to students saying things like the following during office hours: "You mentioned on my draft that page 3 needs more evidence. I checked and I didn't really use quotes or examples on that page. How can I improve page 3?"

Focusing on how to make a product or outcome the best it can be helps everyone involved focus on the goal. By bringing our attention to the needs of the "product," we also take attention (and pressure!) off the individuals in the situation. Focusing on what I call "product over person" helps us focus on goals while simultaneously avoiding creating defensive reactions among readers.

Just as we can build trust, respect, and community through intentional writing, we can also make specific management moves through word choice and arrangement. We can direct, redirect, manage conflict, manage interpersonal difficulties, and more by writing strategically.

Because the truth is: Strategic, intentional writing can impact not only readers' *perceptions* but also their *behaviors.*

Here's a great example:

When I was in college, our trash cans typically said "trash" or "garbage" on them. Today, whenever I visit a college campus, I usually see these bins labeled "landfill." To me, this is a perfect example of strategic writing. This is writing intended to influence not only perceptions but behaviors.

I often bring up this example in live classes, asking, "Why do you think these colleges started labeling their bins this way? What, exactly, is the strategy?"

Participants bring up insights like "Landfill is more visual, more real." Or "'Trash' sounds like you can just make it go away." Or simply, "It implies consequences."

They say they'd be more likely to think twice about "trashing" something when presented with language used in this way. The word "landfill" creates something tangible and even visceral. Doing so not only impacts perceptions and opinions but behaviors too.

This example illustrates the way word choice and arrangement can actually impact meaning—and then drive readers to do one thing or another. By applying this concept to management, we can strategically work to drive conflict resolution, solutions to power struggles, and more.

If you're a team lead, you have a role to play in setting a culture for your team, including considerations like morale and how to navigate through interpersonal issues. Strategic writing gives us tools for navigating confusion, defensiveness, and conflict, and for reducing polarization among or within teams.

Writing strategically to provide redirection or manage interpersonal issues may include:

- ⊙ Managing the use of "you" and "your" intentionally, using the "product over person" approach when helpful
- ⊙ Shifting responsibility, credit, or blame with intention to meet a management goal
- ⊙ Using productive phrasing to promote solutions and forward movement
- ⊙ Using the 5 Ws when assigning tasks to ensure you've given complete instructions

Managing use of "you" and "your" with intention

Watch + Learn

Goes with 100-104

When's the last time you received a text or email that made you feel accused, dismissed, or blamed? How did you feel about the writer, or your relationship with that person, after reading that text or email? Even though it's rarely the writer's intention, a message can accidentally sound accusatory, especially given the possibility of misinterpretation.

A colleague shared an example of this recently. He'd been visiting a country and city where he had an old friend, and they'd planned to meet up. "Let's text about the details later," they'd originally agreed, planning to get in touch on the day they'd decided.

My colleague shared that they never did get in touch. They both forgot to text or call! What also felt bad, though, was the text my colleague's old friend had sent a few days later:

"You never texted!"

It was true. Also true, though, was the fact that this friend hadn't texted either! My colleague felt slightly blamed for a situation that actually included oversights from both people.

Even in a simple, day-to-day scenario like the one described above, the words "you" and "your" can really stand out to the reader. As writers, this means we run the risk of making our reader feel defensive—even when it's by mistake!

Most of us never intend to accuse, attack, or offend others in our writing, but the factor we can't fully control is interpretation. We don't know for sure how our readers will interpret a message. For this reason, it's worth getting strategic about how (or whether) we use words known to potentially create defensive reactions or feel hurtful.

When we have something negative, critical, or controversial to discuss, we can shift our focus from the people involved to the product, goal, or deliverable at hand. By focusing on the product or goal, we stay focused and keep moving forward. There's usually no use getting distracted by blame games; it typically just slows down team progress.

Getting strategic with "you/your" use means thinking about psychological factors like motivation, defensiveness, and many of the other emotional impacts of writing. To keep readers motivated, consider shifting your writing's focus from them to the product you both have an interest in making great.

Writing with "Product over Person" Focus

Revise the sentences below to focus on the product/outcome instead of the individual or reader.

BEFORE: You didn't include a timeline in your report's index.

AFTER: The report's index needs a timeline.

1. You didn't provide sources for the statistics in your slide deck.

   _____

2. Your idea doesn't apply to this process.

   _____

3. The interview questions you wrote are too general and abstract.

   _____

4. Your email was confusing.

   _____

5. You forgot to include the insights from Accounting in your presentation.

   _____

6. Why didn't you create a timeline for the report's appendix?

   _____

7. Why were you so quiet in the meeting?

   _____

8. Can we meet about the new client you didn't follow up with last week?

   _____

9. In your internal memo, your research wasn't very credible.

   _____

10. This project hasn't been completed largely due to your inability to manage time.

    _____

Managing responsibility and accountability with intentional writing

The above revisions illustrate the impact intentional writing can have on a reader's perception. As you shifted focus from the person to the product, you increased focus on the goal or deliverable and decreased the chances of an unproductive conversation. We also have one more option for where we can put our focus: on ourselves.

Overall, then, most sentences can focus on one of three things:

- The reader, or reader's work, work habits, or team
- The product itself; the common, shared goal
- The writer, or the writer's organization, team, or other "we"

Although I argued earlier that we often need more other-focus than self-focus in our writing, we'll sometimes benefit from putting the focus on ourselves. Specifically, we can use strategic writing to shift not only focus but *responsibility* onto ourselves, which means taking it off of others. This can occasionally help our readers, especially when we want to ensure we haven't put the entire load of responsibility for a situation onto them.

Imagine you've held an information session about a given topic, and you're following up with participants the next day. Perhaps you send an email blast, intending to offer them a way to learn more. By accident, though, you've made the email sound like the responsibility is entirely on them. For example, maybe you've written something like this:

> *Thank you for attending yesterday's informative session. If you still need more information, you can contact our office through <u>this link</u>.*

If I'd written the above, I might be thinking about how helpful I've been by offering my readers the chance to learn more information! However, if I reread what I've written, I might notice I've left the responsibility for action all in one place: on my reader.

Considering the potential impact of interpretation (or, from the writer's point of view, misinterpretation), I can imagine how my readers might feel upon reading this. They're represented as the ones who learned enough or who didn't. They're the ones who need to reach out. They're the ones at fault if they *still* need more. In short, they're responsible for basically everything—and I'm responsible for nothing.

With this in mind, I might revise the example we discussed above to something like:

> *Thank you for attending yesterday's informative session. We hope we provided the information you need. Please <u>contact us</u> if you would like more information.*

I've now left open the possibility that I have some responsibility regarding how much they learned (or didn't) in the session. My reader and I are now sharing in the effort of reaching our shared goal of transferring information. Let's try a few of these to see how we can intentionally shift responsibility for something as well as shift focus.

Shifting Responsibility through Intentional Word Choice

Revise the sentences below so the focus/responsibility changes from one person or group to another.

BEFORE: Your list of resources was unorganized.

AFTER: I can't find the resource I need on this list.

1. If you had issues with our workshop, please complete our feedback form.

   _____

2. Your edits on the brochure draft didn't make any sense.

   _____

3. If you need help, make sure to consult our FAQ.

   _____

4. Your idea will never work with the new budget constraints.

   _____

5. It has been requested by management that staff reduce time spent per customer.

   _____

6. Submitting time-off requests adds to the load for management during this season.

   _____

7. All applications have been reviewed so if you have not heard back, you won't be interviewed.

   _____

8. How is this Marketing's problem? I thought Outreach was taking care of this.

   _____

9. The new recipes you introduced are confusing the new first-shift bakers.

_____

10. To progress in management, you need to have a thicker skin.

_____

The revisions you made above likely shifted responsibility or negative attention more toward the writer, rather than leaving it all with the reader. Or, in some cases, you may have shifted positive attention to the reader, rather than keeping credit and importance for the writer only.

At this point, however, you may be thinking: "Hey, I thought we were trying to be concise." In some cases, your revisions might have been longer than the original sentences. If this is the case, not to worry. As writers, we must choose specific moments in which to sacrifice concision in favor of relationship-building.

While we can typically be both concise and courteous in writing (as discussed in Chapter 2), it's worth making courtesy priority #1 in some cases. When the situation will potentially create emotion, consider shifting your top priority from concision to empathy with specific sentences.

We can also manage conflict and difficult situations by focusing on solutions. Writing toward the future, and toward the solution, can help readers and teams stay focused on what matters. To do this, we can use "productive phrasing" when discussing negative situations.

Using productive phrasing to navigate difficult situations

When difficult or negative situations come up, we can try to navigate through the situation with a few goals in mind:

- Improving the negative situation
- Fixing any errors or problems
- Creating and implementing a solution
- Protecting or even strengthening relationships in the process

Productive phrasing can help us accomplish these goals. By writing productively and constructively about negative, critical, or difficult situations, we can help keep the focus on the future and on solutions. Using productive phrasing to revise our writing means we focus more on what will work than what won't.

Watch + Learn

Goes with 97-99

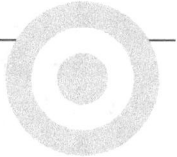

Using productive phrasing does not mean being fake or inauthentic. We can still communicate honest information in an authentic voice while using productive phrasing. The difference? We can honestly talk about what isn't working—but with more focus on how we intend to make it work in the future.

I remember when my younger daughter was getting her driver's license. We went to the DMV multiple times through the process, and people were very helpful every time. On one visit, though, we didn't have the right paperwork. We had just moved from one state in the United States to another, and were still learning what was expected.

"Your daughter can't take the physical test because you don't have the right paperwork," I remember being told.

I then remember saying something like, "OK thanks. What would be our next step then?"

"You don't have the right paperwork, so we can't move her licensing forward."

Hmm.

"I see. What should I do now, to make sure we do get the right paperwork?" I wanted to know.

While we eventually got there, neither of the following felt clear from the original communication:

- Whether it was indeed possible to move forward at this point
- What I'd need to do to fix my mistake and move forward

We can see how communication that doesn't focus on productive outcomes can potentially prevent forward movement. Without clarifying whether—and how—something's possible, we can leave a reader or listener feeling devoid of options.

Productive phrasing takes the same content we want to share, but presents it in a way that orients more toward next steps. For example, here's a before and after based on my experience at the DMV:

> **BEFORE:** We can't give you License A because you didn't provide Form B.

> **AFTER:** Once you provide Form B, you can apply for License A.

What we've done here is taken the "can't" information and turned it into "can" information. It's the same information, just flipped from what hasn't worked so far (in the past) to what *will* or *can* work instead (in the future).

Focusing on Solutions with Productive Phrasing

Revise the sentences below to shift from "can't" information to "can" information.

BEFORE: Applicants may not submit letters of reference until completing their online profile.

AFTER: After completing their online profile, applicants may submit letters of reference.

1. We don't need that information yet because Raul still hasn't given the go-ahead.

_____

2. Please don't share your feedback on the report draft until Felicia has shared first.

_____

3. We don't allow last-minute registrations, so you're out until next month.

_____

4. Don't plant these seedlings next to the tomatoes or eggplant; they don't grow around them.

_____

5. We haven't received the supplies because the distributor used our old address.

_____

6. You can't bring outside food into this establishment or you'll be asked to leave.

_____

7. Since you and Alexa haven't planned for the session, we're postponing you until next week.

_____

8. These glasses aren't the right prescription, so I'm having trouble seeing the data.

_____

9. We haven't received enough applications to start going through them yet.

_____

10. You can't apply for this upgrade without having completed Form 7D and attending an information session.

_____

Using the 5 Ws to ensure giving complete instructions

Finally, even while phrasing things productively, work can't get done if the requirements aren't clear. We can therefore also increase reader response rates by not only phrasing situations positively, but giving complete information.

Watch + Learn

Often, I hear from supervisors who are frustrated at the lack of follow-through when they assign tasks or give instructions to their team members. There are typically two possible reasons when someone doesn't follow through on an instruction:

- The reader didn't read the instructions thoroughly
- The instructions themselves weren't clear—or left out something important

By writing with intention, we can help our team members succeed in tasks we've assigned to them. To do this, we can provide complete information by sharing:

- responsibility
- details about when and where
- a strong command verb representing the assigned action

The easiest way to ensure we've provided all of the above is to revisit the 5 Ws we discussed in Chapter 4. Although every request you write may not need to include all five of the 5 Ws, it's likely that you'll at least want to include:

- **Who** is responsible/accountable
- **What** they need to do (command verb)
- **When** and **where** this needs to take place
- In some cases, **why** it's important or required

Using the 5 Ws to Assign Tasks with Complete Information

Revise the sentences below so the assigned tasks include most or all of the 5 Ws.

BEFORE: Can you finish editing this briefing for me?

AFTER: Please share your edits on this briefing before Thursday's meeting, so we can get your department's perspective.

PRACTICE PROBLEMS:

1. We need these reports duplicated and bound.

   _____

2. Make sure you get everyone's opinion on the book cover design options.

   _____

3. We need to know all inventory on these new medications.

   _____

4. Be ready to argue for or against this regulation in the meeting.

   _____

5. Order enough supplies for the new cohort's writing workshop.

   _____

6. Please complete your online profile as a new employee.

   _____

7. He needs five dozen more flowers for the event.

   _____

8. She is still waiting on the dessert menu options.

   _____

9. Let me know your schedule preferences.

   _____

10. Fill out all the forms before our meeting.

    _____

Key Takeaways & Action Items

You can use this page to record your most important insights, and keep track of the things you want to take action on. Reviewing and paraphrasing what you've learned will also help you remember and feel confident about what we've discussed and practiced.

Most impactful insights:

_____

_____

_____

Best strategies, tips, or tricks:

_____

_____

_____

Areas you'll apply these ideas (situations or types of documents/messages):

_____

One-sentence summary that captures the main point of this chapter:

_____

One word or phrase that captures the theme of this chapter: _____

"Before and After" Examples:

Before: _____

_____

After: _____

_____

Before: _____

_____

After: _____

_____

Chapter

Providing Actionable, Motivating Written Feedback

"They just told me to do it 'better,'" Francine shared with the class, which was full of new managers preparing to write employee performance reviews for the first time.

"What does 'better' mean?" another participant asked. "I mean, 'better' in what way?"

"Exactly," Francine answered.

Francine truly cared about her work, and as a new manager, wanted to do her best to both support her team and succeed in her own projects. To meet her goals, she looked to her supervisor's feedback for direction. Unfortunately, the feedback she received was often vague and didn't feel actionable.

Providing specific, actionable feedback isn't always easy. While we often have a sense of what a team member could do differently, it's hard to articulate these ideas in a way that provides real steps forward.

Let's look at an example. Which of the following examples would you find easiest to follow if you were given this feedback? That is, which really lets you know *what to do?*

- ❑ A. You should work on your communication skills.

- ❑ B. One thing that's helped me is to lead with my main point in emails.

- ❑ C. Your emails are pretty good, but not always clear.

- ❑ D. Try leading with your main point in emails; it really helps!

- ❑ E. If you improve your communication skills, you can better position yourself for promotion.

To me, many of these simply lack what I'd call "actionability." If I'm being told to "work on" something, or do it "better," I'm going to wonder things like:

- In what way?
- In which situations?
- How?

Examples B and D provide this kind of information. We know what type of communication we're talking about, and we have a tangible suggestion of what to do. The others could leave a reader wondering exactly what steps to take, or what it would "look like" to follow through.

Example E makes things a little worse still by carrying what could be interpreted as either helpful advice or a veiled threat. This example might leave the reader with not only questions about the content, but about the tone. We want to avoid this kind of ambiguity in feedback.

Clear feedback, then, answers questions like "What does this look like?" It lets the reader know how to move forward and when and where (in what situations) to do so.

Strong feedback is also motivating. By being clear, we offer readers the ability to act; by being motivating, we help them want to do so. And to give feedback that tangibly contributes to growth, we also want our readers to feel trust in us, and therefore in our recommendations.

You may have heard about the "stress hormones" that come up in situations of conflict and the "love hormones" that we get from trust and connection with others. Most of us have experienced both the difficulty of a stressed, distrustful conversation and the ease of a light, trusting conversation.

When we give others feedback, we want them to feel more like they're having the second type of conversation. When our readers and listeners are stressed or defensive, it's less likely they'll be open to learning something new. If they feel demotivated by the way our feedback sounds, we're working against our own goals of helping them grow.

With that in mind, look at the following examples and consider which would make you the most *motivated* to follow the feedback if you were Jayden. (With these examples, I'll use a more formal style of feedback than the previous.)

- ❑ A. Jayden needs to practice better time management.

- ❑ B. Jayden often gets distracted and wastes time.

- ❑ C. To manage their time better, Jayden can try using our internal calendar app.

- ❑ D. By using our daily calendar app, Jayden's time management skills can grow.

- ❑ E. Jayden should use our internal calendar app to be less distracted.

- ❑ F. The calendar app can help Jayden develop more time management skills.

In this case, C, D, E, and F all offer solutions. They have that going for them! We can also look at whether they have any implications that could negatively impact trust. For example, some readers might find E accusatory. D and F both use productive phrasing, helping point to the future *and* specific solutions for Jayden. F even assumes Jayden has *some* time management skills already, which better conveys respect than many of the other options.

Giving useful feedback has implications for morale and retention as well. Recent research shows that for the younger generations currently in the workforce, growth and professional development matter even more than they have in the past. Surveys among younger groups consistently show that being offered support and growth opportunities can factor into whether to accept a new job—and whether to stay.

Strong feedback can promote growth and development and contribute to productive relationships between leaders and team members. This chapter will help you provide feedback that both informs and motivates by:

- showing what the preferred action "looks like"
- using an actionable feedback formula to provide tangible steps forward in formal feedback
- ensuring feedback is respectful and motivating to the reader

Offering steps forward with feedback that shows what a behavior "looks like"

It can be surprisingly easy to write feedback that fails to show what a suggested action would really "look like." For example, although the following may at first appear to provide helpful feedback, it doesn't actually show *how* Jesus is doing well specifically: "Jesus manages his time fairly effectively and communicates well with team leads."

To provide helpful feedback on what someone is doing well, try telling when, where, or in what circumstances they should keep up the good work.

To see this in action, let's look at a revision of the previous example that specifies exactly *how* (in what circumstances) Jesus is doing well: "Jesus manages his time by using Outlook calendar and avoiding the distractions of social media. He also communicates well by updating the team leads weekly via email." This revision is longer, but it's more helpful because it shows Jesus exactly what to keep doing. When it comes to feedback, specificity is often worth sacrificing a little concision.

Showing a reader what a desired action looks like can include adding examples, tools, resources, and situations to our feedback. For example, the Outlook calendar in the example above works as a tool or resource for Jesus. Saying that he updates his team leads "weekly via email" provides information about when and in which situations Jesus succeeds in this way.

 Making Feedback Tangible and Actionable

Revise the sentences below to provide more tangible, actionable information. This may include saying "how," "when," or "where" a reader can (or does) take a specific action. You may also want to share examples or provide particular resources or tools for improvement.

BEFORE: You should make sure you get to meetings on time.

AFTER: I'd like you to set reminders for meetings with our calendar tool.

1. Your data entry record was much less accurate this month than last month.

   _____

2. Nice job in there.

   _____

3. The tardiness needs to stop.

   _____

4. We were really glad we had you on the committee.

_____

5. Other employees have mentioned that your gossiping can create mistrust.

_____

6. This fact sheet was supposed to include more on the new facility updates.

_____

7. It's great having you be so supportive of the team.

_____

8. We can't have the supplies arriving late again.

_____

9. Rachelle does a great job in client meetings.

_____

10. Brenda needs to show greater commitment to our internal value of honest and open communication.

_____

Using a feedback-writing formula to provide a "how-to" and steps forward

Watch + Learn

If you're concerned about whether the feedback you give feels actionable enough on the reader's end, I'd like to offer a specific writing formula. This formula ensures feedback includes not only what to do (or not do), but how to do it. In live workshops on writing performance reviews, participants who've tried this formula after past sessions report it helps them generate writing that's evidence-based and empowering.

The formula is written for formal feedback—starting with the reader's name. However, we can also adapt the formula to work in more informal feedback situations, like one-on-ones, team huddles, emails, online comments, and more. You can also use this formula in either positive or critical situations; it helps us show what someone's doing well, or what they need to do differently. Here's the formula:

Who + What + [by] How

Simple enough, right? The key here is the use of the word "by," which then prompts us to add the How. Here's how this might work when providing either positive feedback or describing areas of opportunity:

- Tran makes members feel heard by making eye contact and taking notes while they describe their concerns.
- Tran can make members feel more heard by making eye contact and taking notes while they describe their concerns.
- Christie helps her team build community by encouraging team members to share during team huddles.
- Christie can help her team build more community by encouraging team members to share during team huddles.

We can also adapt this formula to help us write actionable feedback in less formal situations. In these cases, our Who will become "You," either stated explicitly or just implied, as in an instruction like "Click here."

"You"/Implied "You" + What + [by] How

For example, when giving feedback in more informal writing situations (like emails, DMs, or on inter-office communication platforms), we might apply this adapted formula in one of these ways:

- You get so many responses because your emails are so clear.
- You might get more responses by clarifying the call to action in the emails.
- Great job supporting the team by mentoring not one, but two new recruits this year.
- Next year, consider boosting your support by signing up to mentor a new recruit.

Using a Writing Formula to Provide Actionable Feedback

Revise the sentences below to follow the Who + What + [by] How formula.

BEFORE: Anzu is positive and helpful and she helps keep morale high on the team.

AFTER: Anzu helps build team morale by asking newer team members how their day is going and offering help when they have questions.

BEFORE: Bertrand needs to show better follow-through after our one-on-ones.

AFTER: Bertrand can follow-up more consistently after one-on-ones by taking notes on required action items.

1. Priya should follow all procedures accurately when creating Onboarding materials.

   _____

2. Ralph needs to better judge when to share information with leadership.

   _____

3. Trina shares need-to-know information with leadership, which is great, but doesn't need to share nice-to-know information so often.

   _____

4. Liz hasn't been using the calendar tool, so it's hard to know when to meet with her.

   _____

5. Elias covered for two other employees who had sick family members.

_____

6. Claire has been shy with her team and needs to build more community.

_____

7. Mira did a great job helping with the interview committee.

_____

8. Clayton is really well-organized and has helped his supervisor keep client files better organized.

_____

9. Sheena can show better customer service skills in both phone calls and emails.

_____

10. Terrence provided assistance to the IT team when he worked overtime last month.

_____

Writing motivating, empowering, and respectful feedback

Clear feedback helps our readers know what to do or not do. Respectful, empowering, and motivating feedback inspires their follow-through. By considering tone as well as content, we can provide feedback that's tangible and actionable—and also makes the reader feel respected and ready to get started. By using motivating phrasing in feedback, we also prevent the kinds of unproductive conversations that can happen when readers feel hurt or defensive.

The comparison below shows how and why some feedback can feel more motivating than others for the reader.

MORE MOTIVATING
"Sheila can meet deadlines more consistently by using her calendar and to-do list daily."
Avoids accusing
Assumes some deadlines met
Provides ways forward
Provides actionable suggestions

LESS MOTIVATING
"Sheila can meet deadlines more consistently by avoiding distraction."
What kind of distraction?
Who says she's distracted?
How do we know for sure?
What should she do, specifically?

The previous example illustrates the way more, or less, motivating feedback can sound to a reader. To make sure your feedback motivates (or at a minimum, doesn't demotivate) your reader, consider the list of best practices below:

MORE EMPOWERING	LESS EMPOWERING
Uses constructive language	Uses reductive or "blamey" language
Talks about what can be done	Talks about what went wrong
Assumes the best	Fails to assume the best
Acknowledges prior efforts	Doesn't address prior efforts
Only discusses what's demonstrable	Includes comments about things we can't demonstrate/prove
Uses objective, fair language	Uses subjective language or opinion
Provides a path forward	Focuses on the past

 Providing Meaningful, Motivating Feedback through Intentional Language

Revise the sentences below to increase potential motivation for the reader, or to reduce any demotivating language you see. Consult the table above for tips on making the feedback examples more empowering.

BEFORE: I don't know why you did it that way.

AFTER: Can you share your thought process?

BEFORE: Carlos needs to communicate with management.

AFTER: Carlos can communicate more consistently with management to build relationships.

1. Katie can improve workplace relationships by showing more emotional intelligence.

   _____

2. Watch your nonverbals in there!

   _____

3. One way to be less nervous in meetings is to write down ideas ahead of time.

   _____

4. Can you make your email updates more specific?

   _____

5. Make sure you're not getting behind on those board reports.

_____

6. Dinesh needs to improve his accuracy rate and avoid so many errors.

_____

7. Leslie's communication would be improved with more attention to her readers or listeners.

_____

8. Ricardo is a good account processor.

_____

9. Troy doesn't give his team useful feedback often enough.

_____

10. That's not the right way to approach the project.

_____

Key Takeaways & Action Items

You can use this page to record your most important insights, and keep track of the things you want to take action on. Reviewing and paraphrasing what you've learned will also help you remember and feel confident about what we've discussed and practiced.

Most impactful insights:

_____

_____

_____

Best strategies, tips, or tricks:

_____

_____

_____

Areas you'll apply these ideas (situations or types of documents/messages):

_____

One-sentence summary that captures the main point of this chapter:

_____

One word or phrase that captures the theme of this chapter: _____

"Before and After" Examples:

Before: _____

_____

After: _____

_____

Before: _____

_____

After: _____

_____

10

Writing with Executive Presence

When Emily Sander (in this case, her real name!) interviewed me on her podcast *Leveraging Leadership*, we discovered we had something in common. Looking back, we realized we'd each used language with the potential to reduce our perceived confidence and capabilities earlier in our careers.

In Emily's case, she'd had to pay special attention to her language use when she first joined the C-suite. I told her I'd had to do the same as I grew in my career: watch my word choice to make sure I wasn't "underselling" myself or representing myself without enough respect or confidence.

We discussed the way we used to write messages that didn't represent our inner confidence that well.

"I'd find a lot of apologies or sort of 'guilty' comments like 'If it's not too much trouble,'" Emily explained.

"Yep. For me, it was the words 'just' and 'only,'" I added. "'Just an idea, but...,'" I went on. "Or 'only a thought, but...'"

Over the years, Emily reoriented her writing to project confidence, and to inspire it in others. She served as a chief of staff in big tech. She became a successful author and coach who now helps executives, founders, and other leaders lead with confidence. By reflecting on our language use and getting intentional with word choice, we can all drive our own success by representing ourselves with confidence and self-respect.

Depending on your upbringing and what cultural expectations and norms you've been immersed in, you may have developed a habit of sounding less confident in your writing than you really are. Part of writing with what we might call "executive presence" includes both projecting and inspiring confidence.

Watch + Learn

Ideally, we also want our own confidence to help others feel confident. We can create confidence on the part of our readers with intentional writing. And we can write in a way that empowers our readers and those we write about. Empowering others through word choice can become a tool of servant leadership.

On the other hand, as discussed in Chapter 6, we don't want our writing to suggest that we're always self-focused. We don't want to cruise right past confident to arrogant! This is yet another need for balance in writing.

The truth is, we can both respect others through our writing and respect ourselves through our writing. And we can do both simultaneously. We can share our thoughts confidently while also treating our readers well and representing anyone we write about with strength and empowerment.

We saw in Chapter 8 how intentional writing can impact power dynamics. Writing with executive presence means empowering both ourselves and our readers. So, we'll project confidence but also inspire it in others. We'll share our knowledge while respecting that of our readers at the same time.

To write with executive presence, let's practice the following:

- Projecting confidence by avoiding self-reducing language and getting to the action quickly

- Inspiring confidence by providing a complete picture and being transparent about what we do or don't know

- Intentionally empowering or amplifying others by the way we write about them

Before we get started, take a moment to reflect on your writing's confidence level.

 Conveying Confidence through Writing

Reflect on your "default" writing style. Check the box next to the description that rings true for you.

My writing usually sounds:

❑ More confident than my speaking

❑ Less confident than my speaking

❑ About the same as my speaking in terms of confidence level

Action-oriented language that doesn't "self-reduce" makes us sound confident

Which of the following would make you think I'm confident about how to proceed in a hypothetical discussion about reporting on data?

Watch + Learn

- In my opinion, we might also want to scrutinize the data from the last annual cycle.
- Let's analyze last year's data too.
- Let's look at last year's data too.

I'm guessing it's one of the second two. The first version not only relies on slow lead-ins and showy words, but it reduces its own power through self-dismissive language at the same time. These writing choices make the sentence simultaneously less concise and less confident. The big vocab words just weren't enough to make up for the self-reducing language. In fact, they may have made it even more obvious.

Let's dissect these three areas and identify how to write in a way that emphasizes our confidence and capabilities. Here are the three writing moves that can reduce the confident tone in our writing:

- *Using slow lead-ins.* By delaying information for our readers, we can sound unsure of what we want to say, or less committed to what we're saying. Slow lead-ins also postpone the action part of our sentences, which means readers not only have to wait, but may think we aren't action-oriented.

- *Using showy words.* By choosing showy words when they aren't necessary, writers can risk looking more uncertain—or even insecure—than they would by using more familiar synonyms. It's a little like the idea that if you have to flaunt it, do you really have it?

- *Self-reducing or self-dismissing.* By using reductive language, "maybe" language, or words like "only" or "just," we risk reducing or even dismissing the power of our own words—and thus our own power. Words that diminish our work like "small," "a bit," or "little" can also have this impact.

To sound more confident and convey more authority, we can do the opposite of the previous three writing moves. We can get right to the action, use familiar, unthreatening words, and make sure we don't self-dismiss. Here's an example of each:

Watch + Learn

- *Get right to the action.* By avoiding slow lead-ins, we can get right to the point. Then, make sure your action word (verb) is strong and visual.

  BEFORE: I'm writing to suggest that we talk to last year's vendor first.

  AFTER: Let's consult last year's vendor first.

- *Use familiar words.* Using familiar words helps us look like we don't have to "show it" when we're confident—we just are.

  BEFORE: It is a requirement that we obtain a new vendor to provide procured services like training materials and live workshops.

  AFTER: We need a new vendor for our training materials and live workshops.

- *Avoid self-reducing.* When presenting your view, avoid phrases like "It's just an idea, but…" or "Only my thoughts, but…"

  BEFORE: If it isn't inconvenient, I would like to suggest that we consider more local vendors.

  AFTER: Let's look for more local vendors.

  OR: Are there local vendors we can consider?

At this point, it's worth reflecting a little on our pasts. Our communication styles can often depend on our upbringing and social conditioning. We may have been acculturated, or raised, to speak (and write) confidently, and put our ideas forward without hesitation. Or we may have been encouraged to sound more deferential and avoid making ourselves and our statements sound "too big." The habits we develop, then, can depend to some degree on what culture we were raised in, and what roles we were given in that culture.

In live workshops, participants often share about their cultural communication journeys. Typically, participants who were conditioned with norms for a few specific groups feel like they've been raised to not sound confident in writing. Often, comments like this come from participants who feel that either their gender or having been brought up in a culture that emphasizes humility has impacted how bold they sound in writing and speaking.

Humility is typically a good thing, but if you feel you've been raised to speak with too much deference and humility, or to put yourself last too much, try following the advice above. When we write concisely, we automatically sound more confident than when we're wordy. However, if projecting confidence is specifically part of our relational goal as well, we also want to practice specific word choice and sentence arrangement.

Projecting Confidence through Writing

Revise the following sentences to convey confidence by removing slow lead-ins, simplifying the vocabulary, and removing self-reducing language.

BEFORE: In my opinion, the ebooks are preferable.

AFTER: I prefer the ebooks.

1. It's just an idea, but what if we advertise this sooner?

   _____

2. This is to inform you that we will need your materials submitted by Thursday.

   _____

3. We might want to consider asking Maintenance for insights, just an idea.

   _____

4. Only my thoughts, but maybe we need a second meeting to follow up.

   _____

5. Sorry to bother you, but it has been pointed out to me that I need a mentor, and I wanted to ask you.

   _____

6. I'm running my own little business now.

   _____

7. I thought I'd ask last year's vendor, if you think that's a good idea.

   _____

8. I know you're really busy, but if you have time, maybe I could run an idea by you?

   _____

9. Do you think it would make sense for me to consider presenting on Monday?

   _____

10. No worries if this won't work, but I think I'd like to be considered as a presenter.

   _____

By using intention, we can arrange our writing so it respects both us and our readers. We can put ourselves forward with confidence but not arrogance. We can see that others get their needs met—and that we do too.

Inspiring confidence in others with the 5 Ws

Confidence matters on the part of the reader too. If you've ever read something that gives you anxiety, you know what I mean. For me, it's tax documentation. One look and I'm already losing confidence. This means I'm more likely to procrastinate or even make mistakes.

But a confident reader is an active reader. So, it helps to give readers confidence about what they're reading. We want our readers to feel confident about what our message means, and about what to do in terms of following up.

The previous revision exercise helps us hone our writing to represent ourselves as confident, capable people. In addition, though, our message has a better chance of succeeding if our readers feel the same way. By inspiring confidence in our readers, and recognizing their capability, we have a greater chance they'll act on our message. Perhaps more to the point, when we accidentally make our readers feel nervous or insecure, they're less able to respond positively and take action.

To ensure our readers feel confident about our messages, it helps to provide clear, complete information. We can also be transparent about what we do or don't know. Our word choice matters too: accessible language helps us be more inclusive, avoiding alienating readers with language they might find intimidating. Finally, when appropriate, we can use "we"-oriented language that keeps the writer and reader together on "the same side."

When you're writing about a topic that might concern or inspire emotion on the part of your readers, consider using these strategies to ensure your writing helps readers stay confident:

- Give concise, complete information by including the 5 Ws in a Who + What structure.

- Transparently state if you do not know something, rather than trying to avoid it.

- Use accessible language.

- Use "we"-oriented language when appropriate.

Inspiring Confidence through Intentional Writing

Revise the sentences below to:
(1) offer more complete information by including more of the 5 Ws and
(2) use accessible, transparent, "we"-oriented language.

BEFORE: I may be getting bad news from Budgeting.

AFTER: I'll share Budgeting's update with you as soon as I get it in Thursday's meeting.

BEFORE: Leadership is asking for feedback about the survey from each person.

AFTER: Leadership wants written feedback from our whole team by Friday, to help guide next year's survey.

1. The Wellness team will offer fitness check-ins.

   _____

2. The head chef wants to change two of our recipes.

   _____

3. I'd like to hear everyone's schedule preferences right away.

   _____

4. The event planning is going well but we need more outreach.

   _____

5. This product hasn't been selling very well.

   _____

6. Headquarters has hinted at cutbacks.

   _____

7. I'd like you to present to the committee to build speaking confidence.

   _____

8. The new cover design isn't popular with everyone.

   _____

9. The electrician hasn't signed off on the wiring, so we're not ready.

   _____

10. Facilities let me know that we've been wasting power by leaving devices on at night.

_____

Inspiring confidence by amplifying others

We can also inspire confidence by building up others through the way we write or speak about them. Instead of saying someone "was in charge" of a project, for example, we can say they "directed" or "supervised" it. By sharing about the expertise of others, we not only make them look confident and capable, but convey a sense of our own confident leadership as well.

Watch + Learn

Team leads can use intentional amplification to help inspire and develop particular team members. Part of having executive presence is knowing how to provide servant leadership—supporting one's team as a leader. Writing to amplify others helps leaders support their teams in this way.

Any of us who work on teams can also make agreements with a colleague to intentionally amplify one another. Imagine the impact if people consistently read about you "directing" and "supervising," instead of "was-ing"! Whether or not you're a team lead, you can use the ideas below to help support and build up others.

A few ways to amplify others through intentional writing include:

- Using powerful verbs to represent actions
- Ensuring they get the Who spot of the sentence
- Showing evidence of their expertise

Inspiring Confidence by Amplifying Others

Revise the sentences to amplify the person referenced. Make sure you use a powerful, visual verb to represent this person's actions and abilities.

BEFORE: I asked Linda to take on the data management.

AFTER: Linda will manage our data collection.

1. One of the recommendations we might consider is Bethany's.

   _____

2. Carlos was really good at explaining the process to his team.

   _____

3. I have selected Shaundra to be the go-to person on that project.

   _____

4. I learned how to be a good listener from Jay in Accounting.

   _____

5. Dominique in Marketing does all their writing and does it well.

   _____

6. Kat seems to know a lot about this; let's ask her.

   _____

7. I was able to see Rebecca as a mentor during my first year.

   _____

8. Tam did a nice job sketching out designs for our remodel.

   _____

9. This idea actually came from Raul, who's experienced in IT innovation.

   _____

10. One of the people in Facilities, Darlene, is super helpful.

   _____

Key Takeaways & Action Items

You can use this page to record your most important insights, and keep track of the things you want to take action on. Reviewing and paraphrasing what you've learned will also help you remember and feel confident about what we've discussed and practiced.

Most impactful insights:

_____

_____

_____

Best strategies, tips, or tricks:

_____

_____

_____

Areas you'll apply these ideas (situations or types of documents/messages):

_____

One-sentence summary that captures the main point of this chapter:

_____

One word or phrase that captures the theme of this chapter: _____

"Before and After" Examples:

Before: _____

_____

After: _____

_____

Before: _____

_____

After: _____

_____

How to Use this Workbook with Your Class or Team

If you're an educator or a team lead, you can easily use this workbook as a learning tool for your participants or team members. Teachers and trainers can ask participants to complete a chapter's practice exercises individually or in groups, and then facilitate discussions about application areas. Team leads can assign chapters or practice exercises in regular meetings, adding to your team's focus on clear, engaged, and respectful writing.

Watch + Learn

To help you use this workbook with your class or team, I'll provide discussion questions for each of the chapters below. Then, I'll offer ideas for incorporating this workbook into any of the following situations:

- ⦿ business writing classes or workshops in academic or business settings
- ⦿ leadership development programs in organizations
- ⦿ as a supervisor—in weekly or monthly team meetings, huddles, one-on-ones, or all-hands sessions.

If you'd like, check out the welcome video that provides an overview of the process described in the coming pages.

Chapter Discussion Questions

Consider using these questions to facilitate either whole-group discussions or small-group activities. You'll find questions that may work best either before or after completing a given chapter's practice exercises. Some questions may be more conducive to a corporate or academic setting, a leadership program, or an all-hands discussion. Below the questions, I'll provide tips for using the discussion questions in each type of environment.

Chapter	Pre-chapter Discussion Questions	Post-chapter Discussion Questions
1	Reflecting on your typical approach to writing, what do you already do that you want to keep doing? Reflecting on your typical approach to writing, what do you wish you could do differently?	After studying your own writing defaults, list 2-3 goals you have for your writing. Based on your reflections about your writing style, what's an example of a writing choice that would work for some readers but not others?
2	Do you consider yourself a wordy writer, a direct writer, or somewhere in between? In your work area, when are you impacted by having to read material that requires a high cognitive load? What are some examples of materials you've read that require too much time or effort from the reader?	In what writing situations could the strategies in this chapter help make your writing more clear and concise? What documents or messages does your team or department create that currently require a high cognitive load from readers? Which strategies might help those documents/messages require a reduced cognitive load from readers?
3	What barriers have you faced in getting your messages read, responded to, and acted on? In what types of situations have you sent messages that either get ignored or followed up on late? What strategies do you use to make your writing clear and impactful so it gets read and answered?	What documents or emails do you write that could benefit from being more scannable? Which written products (newsletters, websites, documents, etc.) does your team or organization produce that could benefit from using simpler word choice? Who are the readers of these products?
4	When emailing, how do you typically clarify your main point, and where in your email do you do this? When you ask your reader to take action, how do you usually present your "call to action"?	How might you apply the two-part subject line in your work area? In which situations, and with which readers, do you think this will help? How could your team or organization use the 3-step emailing process to save time among the group—for both writers and readers?

5	Which documents or messages do you write, or read, that can be hard for a reader to "navigate"? Many readers enjoy reading something written with "flow." Have you come across a piece of reading that either flowed well or notably did not flow? What was the result for you as a reader?	Which documents or messages that you work on could benefit from the flow process described in this chapter? Which documents or messages that you write could benefit from using clear topic sentences?
6	How have you been impacted by tone in messages you've read? For example, have you ever felt immediately motivated or immediately upset after reading a message? What happened in that message to create this relational impact?	In what situations might you use this chapter's strategies for building trust and respect? If you're a leader or manager, how might you encourage people on your team to write in a way that builds respect and belonging?
7	Who are some of the readers you write to most often? What preferences have you discovered about the way they like to receive information? What are some of the communication norms or expectations in the field you're working or studying in? Do you think your communication style has been impacted by any of the cultures you belong to (generational, industry, regional, ethnic, etc.)? If so, in what ways? What differences have you noticed between the communication norms of your cultures and those of colleagues from different cultures? (This might be generational cultures, norms of different industries, or even regional or ethnic cultures.)	After reflecting on some of your readers' potential communication expectations, what might you do differently in your writing going forward? If you're a leader or manager, what communication style differences have you observed among your team? In which cases might you attribute these differences to individual or group communication norms? If you're a leader or manager, how might you encourage people on your team to write in a way that considers their readers' cultures and communication expectations?

8	Have you ever felt disrespected by a message you received (or by the writer of that message)? What factors in the writing made you feel this way? Have you ever felt accused after receiving a specific message? What aspect of the message made you feel this way?	In what kinds of conversations might you apply the concepts of "product over person" and/or "productive phrasing" in your writing or speaking? If you're a leader or manager, how could this chapter's "product over person" and/or "productive phrasing" strategies help build harmony among your team? If you're a leader or manager, how might you encourage people on your team to write toward productivity and collaboration, even when facing potential conflict with customers or clients?
9	What type of feedback do you provide in your role—formal, informal, or both? When providing feedback, what's the most difficult: making sure it's tangible, keeping the tone motivational, or providing next steps?	In what situations might you apply the feedback writing formula from this chapter? How can you apply the strategies in this chapter to informal feedback opportunities like conversations, emails, or one-on-ones? If you're a leader or manager, how might you encourage people on your team to provide feedback that's actionable and motivating?
10	How confident do you feel you sound in your writing? What obstacles to confident communication have you faced in the past? If you're a leader or manager, have you observed people on your team whose writing doesn't reflect their inner confidence?	Do you feel that your upbringing or the cultures you've lived in have impacted how confident you sound in writing or speaking? Which strategies for confident writing do you think you'll apply to your writing going forward? What opportunities do you have in your role to amplify others? If you're a leader or manager, how might you encourage people on your team to write in a way that represents them as confident?

Tips for using this workbook in academic or corporate business writing classes

Teachers and trainers can use this workbook, and many of the provided discussion questions, to create class activities and discussions. I recommend providing pre-chapter questions as homework or small group discussion topics, and then facilitating larger discussions with the post-chapter questions.

Whether you teach in an academic setting or train in a corporate or public sector setting, I recommend approaching the workbook in two parts: chapters 1-5 and then chapters 6-10. This will allow you to focus on discussing informational goals with the first set of chapters and relational goals with the second. Separating the two chunks in this way can help make the content easier for learners to recognize, categorize, and integrate into their daily practices.

Depending on what environment you teach in, I'd suggest scheduling your chapter discussions and exercises as follows:

- **Business settings:** Consider holding two separate sessions or workshops, one focused on chapters 1-5 and another focused on chapters 6-10. Or, assign specific practice exercises that apply to specific learner work areas, and then review possible revisions together. In some cases, you might have "all staff" complete chapters 1-5 only, and then hold a separate session for leaders, discussing chapters 6-10.
- **Academic settings:** Consider assigning one chapter per week, including both reading and practice exercises. Then, discuss and review the exercises the following week. You can use the pre-chapter discussion questions to create interest before learners read and complete a given chapter, and then follow up with a post-chapter question in the next class meeting.

Tips for using this workbook in leadership development programs in organizations

Internal leadership development programs can help emerging leaders communicate with confidence by discussing both the informational and relational goals of writing. If you facilitate a program for new leaders, consider adding a module called Strategic Writing for Leaders. Then, you can assign the workbook in halves (first half on clarity and concision goals, second half on relational goals) and hold two sessions in which you discuss application.

Here's how I'd recommend approaching this:

Session 1: Writing for Today's Readers. Ask your leadership development participants to complete chapters 1-5 before the session. Or ask them to skim the narrative portion but skip the exercises. You can then have them do exercises in groups during the session.

- Focus on how they as leaders can both write for today's readers and encourage their teams to do so.

Homework between sessions: Ask your participants to use the time between sessions to observe the following:

- the writing choices made in messages they receive (Example: "This writer put their call to action at the bottom of the email.")
- their own reactions to those writing choices. (Example: "I noticed myself getting frustrated as a result.")

Session 2: Writing to Build and Manage Relationships. Require chapters 6-10 for your second session. Or have participants prepare by reading the narrative ahead, and then assign groups to do the practice problems.

- Focus on practice for providing feedback, writing to build respect, and writing to manage conflict or team disagreement.

Tips for using this workbook as a supervisor

Supervisors can use this workbook to build communication skills among direct reports while also helping teams save time and build respect and camaraderie. You can assign an exercise or a chapter to individuals, or to the whole team, and then discuss in standing meetings. To target skill gap areas you've observed in your team, consider assigning exercises or whole chapters in one of these ways:

- Survey the team before starting, asking which writing problems they deal with most as readers. Then, assign chapters or exercises that address those problems specifically. For example, maybe team members say something like, "When I read messages from the team, sometimes I'm not sure if I need to do anything, or just know about it." You can then assign the activity on writing a clear call to action.

- Group the team into specific learning areas depending on their roles. Then, assign sections based on their responsibilities. For example, you might assign:
  - Chapter 8's conflict resolution strategies for customer-facing employees
  - Chapter 9's feedback formula for new managers
  - Chapter 2's concision strategies for new employees who are still becoming familiar with the norms of business writing

- Work through the chapters in order, asking individuals on your team to be responsible for specific practice exercises. Then ask the entire team to complete those exercises, allowing the responsible team member to facilitate this discussion.

Finally, if you know people on your team learn well through visuals or video, consider pairing a chapter or practice exercise with one of the videos referenced with a QR code. You could watch the video together as a team, then ask team members to complete the practice exercises in that section.

ACKNOWLEDGMENTS

This workbook is about the way writing impacts people, and so many people helped in its creation by sharing their insights and perspectives with me over the years. I am, as always, indebted to the people I've met in my classes, for what they've taught me and helped me realize about both writing and how to teach writing. From the early days of teaching highschool and college English, to more recent projects with public and private sector clients, it's always been the participants who've shown me what works and what doesn't.

As I collected my thoughts for this workbook, many others helped me with the process in specific ways. Paul Briley offered coworking sessions which helped me keep moving forward. Kelly Mieske provided user perspectives and suggestions from the reader's point of view. Anne Janzer showed me that I too could learn the ways of publishing, distributing, and marketing my book independently.

As the concepts and activities came together into chapters, I leaned on a talented editing and design team to help me see the best ways of presenting my content. Skylar Griego once again offered incisive editorial advice that made the workbook's explanations and practice exercises that much better. Guy Rogers helped me turn my curriculum into a truly useful learning product through his insights about the ways design decisions impact reading, thinking, and learning.

This workbook offers a new way of learning, in that it pairs reading and practice exercises with optional video instruction—including the opportunity to leave questions for the author in a live format on YouTube. I have Sunshine Chen and Linda Whittaker of Sunshine Creative Agency to thank for much of this. They inspired me to start the High-Value Writing YouTube channel and taught me how. In doing so, they helped me see connections in my work that have translated to expanded learning opportunities for my students, viewers, and readers.

Finally, a huge thank you to Christopher Nettles, who helped proofread the workbook and has helped me in countless other ways through his work at High-Value Writing and general wonderfulness as a person. Thank you all for your support in creating this workbook that I hope will now empower people all over the world.

ABOUT THE AUTHOR

Erin Lebacqz is an award-winning educator who teaches Strategic Writing in the private and public sectors. Her YouTube channel @highvaluewriting and book *High-Value Writing: Real World Strategies for Real-World Writing* help learners write with intention and confidence.

Erin is also the founder of High-Value Writing LLC, which offers virtual and in-person workshops, as well as on-demand e-courses on writing with clarity and impact in the workplace. Erin lives in Sacramento, California.

To learn more about Erin's work, or to book her to speak or conduct a workshop for your team, visit www.highvaluewriting.com.